Theme Park Design

Behind The Scenes With An Engineer

By Steve Alcorn

Theme Perks Inc.
Orlando, FL

First Printing, October 2010

Theme Perks Press
www.themeperks.com

Printed in the United States of America

Acknowledgments

Thanks to the employees of Alcorn McBride Inc, who for more than twenty-five years have devoted themselves to making themeparks reliable, fun and exciting. I'm blessed to have a staff of such special people.

Thanks also to screenwriter Doran William Cannon, who encouraged me to create this text, originally part of the course now offered at imagineeringclass.com.

Finally, thanks to all of the Imagineers I've worked with over the years. Your creativity and professionalism are what make this profession so special.

Dedication

To my wife Linda, for dragging me kicking and
screaming into this whole, crazy theme park thing. It's
been quite a ride.

Table of Contents

Chapter 1: Don't Panic... Yet

Beep! Beep! Beep!

Something big—really big—and yellow was backing towards me, churning up sand and flinging it in all directions as it sought purchase on the giant mound of dirt. I was pretty sure the driver couldn't see me through the wire mesh of his rear window, and I was certain he wouldn't have stopped anyway. He had a mountain to move, and it was my job to not get killed when he went Beep! Beep! Beep!

My feet slid deep into the loose dirt as I scaled the side of the mound, trying to get out of his way. Sand filled my steel-toed construction shoes and I cursed. Struggling higher, I finally crested the pile and stood surveying the Martian-like landscape from thirty feet above.

There was mud everywhere. Except where there were mountains of sand. On each mountain earth movers crawled, shepherding them like giant yellow dung beetles.

Looming over me was the immense, silver geodesic sphere of Spaceship Earth—the big ball, the construction workers called it. Now that I was underneath, it looked impossibly large.

For months I'd watched Spaceship Earth take shape from across the park. It had started as an ugly mass of steel. Then tiny silver triangles were attached to the dark metal framework, slowly turning into a cap, then a Pac-man, and finally the world's largest golf ball. Now, beneath it, I discovered those "tiny" silver triangles were each the size of my car.

Speaking of my car, a half an hour earlier, at the edge of the construction site, I had started on the seemingly short walk from where I parked it. In future years this same walk—on immaculate, rosy pavement—would take me two minutes. But on the construction site, time and distance and size bent in strange ways that seemed to violate some fundamental law.

Beep! Beep! Beep! My attention turned back to my pursuer. The thing was hungrily gobbling up half of my mountain so I hurried down the slipping sand and splattered through a truck-sized mud-hole to the stairway.

I was here to find the rep from the electric motor company. We needed him over at American Adventure, where our carriage wouldn't move, its motor silenced by a balky control cabinet. But he was here at Spaceship Earth where his troubles loomed even larger.

Puffing at the top of the second—or was it the third?—flight of stairs, I struggled to make out recognizable objects in the tangled jumble of black steel. It wasn't easy. Ride track corkscrewed crazily up and out of sight, chased by a lunatic's stairway and surrounded by random steel cross bracing. Everything was painted flat black.

The track was studded with motors and drive wheels, more being added every day in an attempt to convince the endless chain of vehicles to climb that crazy hill to its crest, then descend to the bottom and do it all over again. It was an incredibly heavy pearl necklace being dragged around a Dali-inspired escalator.

The set designers were supervising the carpenter who was installing 1950s furniture as I puffed my way up the downramp. Backward in time I climbed. There's the library at Alexandria. There's Pompeii. There's the Greek Theater. I'd seen these set pieces being fabricated in a warehouse in Tujunga months before, and two years earlier I'd walked through a miniature, eye-level mockup of the whole thing. Now it was like a double dose of deja vu.

Farther up—pant, pant—construction workers were jockeying a $30,000 control cabinet around a corner, trying to figure out how to get it through an equipment room doorway that had ended up blocked by a stair railing which wasn't on the plans. I grimaced as I watched them handle it with the same care usually reserved for bags of fertilizer or airport luggage.

There were only worklights installed so far, but the lighting designers were dodging welding sparks, directing someone high overhead to install the steel pipes that would hold the theatrical fixtures.

The only engineers I passed were audio people. They were sitting in a vehicle watching a guy with a screwdriver and chisels remove the on-board sound equipment for the second or third time. The new motors had interfered with the audio underpinnings during the brief moment the vehicles had moved; the audio system looked like a crumpled tin can.

All around me was activity: the bustle of construction workers, the stench of the welding torches, the cacophony of hammer against steel. It was heaven.

I found the electric motor rep working under the track and we eventually made it back to mud-hole level. Outside the Project Manager was looking for his car. He'd parked it right over there. I knew the spot well. I'd already climbed over that mound of dirt on my way in.

Opening day was barely two months away.

Would we be done?

$$***$$

Welcome to my world. It's a world balanced precariously between surreal creativity and gritty reality. A world where brainstorms turn into contraptions. A world where fun is a business, and—if we're lucky—business is fun.

I'm Steve Alcorn, CEO of Alcorn McBride Inc., a company that engineers equipment for theme parks all over the world. For nearly thirty years I've been designing audio, video, show and lighting control equipment for themed attractions. It's been great fun bringing hundreds—perhaps thousands—of attractions to life all over the world. Now I'd like to share some of that experience with you. During the course of this book we'll even design an attraction, or perhaps a whole theme park.

Don't worry, you don't need to know calculus, Boyle's law or what cement is made from in order to enjoy this journey. We won't be using math, chemistry or computer programming.

So who is this book for?

Two sets of people, really. It's aimed at those who are considering a career in any area having to do with themed entertainment. And it's aimed at anyone who has ever gone to a theme park and wondered, "How did they do that?"

This book describes the different types of attractions found in theme parks, and how they work. It also surveys the many diverse engineering fields involved in designing theme park attractions, and explains what technical curriculum you should pursue to qualify for those jobs.

As theme park designers, we'll concentrate on what it takes to accomplish our technical goals in every area—architecture, ride control, show control, audio, video, electrical, lighting, mechanical, acoustics, hydraulics, even ergonomics. And just like in the real world, we'll be sticking our nose into other peoples' business! We'll evaluate art direction, attendance, concessions, food service, marketing, throughput, and return on investment, at least as they relate to Theme Park Design.

You can use the knowledge you gain here to conceptualize a park and its attractions, and to determine what it would take to create that park—and you won't need a stock of Twinkies and coffee to help you work 24 hours a day. (But you may want to stock up on Twinkies anyway.)

This book covers three broad areas: people, attractions, and disciplines. You'll learn about the people who create and operate theme parks, the different types of attractions and how they work, and about different engineering fields and related disciplines involved in theme park design.

By the time you've finished this book you will understand theme parks better as a guest. For those interested in a career in theme park engineering, you'll have an idea of the different disciplines that you may chose from, and the types of knowledge you'll need to qualify for those positions.

The Accidental Engineer

I ended up a theme park engineer by accident. It all started when my wife was in the third grade. Really.

You see, that's when she decided that when she grew up she was going to design rides for Disneyland. She started with a piece of plywood she covered with little trees and cardboard buildings, making a scale model of the whole park. It even had a tiny little Skyway, with droplets of clay dangling from a copper wire.

I came along later. Much later.

As a college student and inveterate electronic tinkerer, I started a company that made microcomputers before IBM invented something called the PC. Newly married to this woman determined to design rides for Disneyland, the pull of theme parks was strong. Upon graduating she interviewed with exactly one company: Walt Disney Imagineering (then called WED Enterprises). She was hired to help design Epcot, and within two years she was the Electronic Project Engineer on a half dozen attractions. Talk about a trial by fire.

Surrounded by theme park engineers, I was inevitably drawn in. Called in as an outside consultant (a "guru from afar") to help with the particularly complex American Adventure attraction, I set out on a two-week business trip to Florida. Two years later, I came home.

But once you've had a nibble, you're hooked.

And that's how I ended up a theme park engineer by accident.

***

Of course, not everyone who helps create theme parks is a theme park engineer. Theme park engineers work with many other disciplines to accomplish their jobs. I'll be mentioning them as we interact with them.

We'll start by looking at people. People are a theme park's most important asset.

It takes people to create a theme park; that's what this book is about. But it also takes people to operate a theme park: to run the rides, keep them working, keep it clean, and keep it stocked with interesting merchandise and palatable food. As theme park engineers, we need to design our park with these people in mind. In a sense, they are our customers. If they can't run their park efficiently, we haven't done our jobs right.

Of course, there's an even more important group of people: our guests. Everything we put into our theme park needs to be designed with them in mind. Our theme park must lure them in, and keep them coming back, or there will be no one to pay the bills!

The next few chapters look at these groups of people. By understanding each of them we'll be able to design a better park.

Chapter 2: Be My Guest

It was a beautiful late January day at Disneyland. The air was crisp, but sitting on a sunny bench outside Pirates of the Caribbean my wife and I didn't need our jackets. The plaza between New Orleans Square and the Rivers of America stretched in front of us, an acre of rose-colored pavement nearly devoid of people. A young girl tugged her mother across the plaza toward Haunted Mansion, as an older woman, probably her grandmother, hurried to keep up. Two middle-aged women with shopping bags strolled past, headed in the direction of Adventureland.

For a moment the entire plaza was empty. Then a family of four came into view, heading in our direction. The mother held the hand of a small boy, perhaps four years old, while his six-year-old sister led the way. She pointed excitedly at the entrance to Pirates, and her brother did an admirable imitation of a hyperactive poodle. Twenty feet behind, their father trudged up the hill, hand planted in his pockets, a wire dangling from his ear, and a scowl on his face.

What's going on here? Have you guessed? Where are all the people? And why only women and children, and one unhappy man?

It was Super Bowl Sunday, one of the slowest days of the year in most American theme parks.

One of the jobs we'll talk about later is that of forecasting theme park attendance for staffing and budgeting reasons. This little vignette gives you a hint of how difficult that might be. It also illustrates that understanding the demographics of our guests is not a simple task.

Demographics? What's that? It means "background" in every sense of the word. Here are just a few, in order of importance:

- Location of Residence
- Age
- Family Income
- Educational Level
- Race

- Sex
- Religion

There are almost as many types of potential theme park guests as there are types of people in the world. I say "almost" because we can immediately rule out a few categories. Yanamamo tribesmen from the jungles of South America are not very likely to visit our theme park. That seems obvious; I'm instinctively applying selection criteria to narrow and define my audience.

You may already think you know who goes to theme parks: middle class white families from large metropolitan areas. Statistically, if that's your guess, you're right. In the US, they represent a large chunk—although not necessarily even half—of all theme park guests.

There are a few problems with such a simple-minded analysis.

First, we've already assumed that we know what we mean when we say "theme park". I'll bet my definition is a lot broader than yours. To me, a theme park is really any place that offers "dedicated venue" themed attractions. Dedicated venue means that a facility is always used for the same thing. A neighborhood multiplex cinema does not qualify. But a theater that always shows the same film is a dedicated venue. That means that all of the following are themed attractions:

- Museums
- National Park Service Visitor Centers
- Corporate Communications Centers
- Broadcasting Studio Visitor Tours
- Themed Shopping Malls
- Themed Restaurants
- and many more.

Clearly, each of these categories attracts a very different demographic. As designers we need to understand whom we are designing for. A military history museum has completely different attractions and a whole different level of signage than, say, a kids' science exploration center.

A second problem with assuming that our guests are all white middle class families is that it isn't a very accurate descriptor. A park full of roller coasters will appeal to teenagers, but not their parents or younger siblings. Legoland is for the preteen crowd. And Epcot attracts the young and old, but leaves many teenagers unimpressed. As theme park designers we need to understand whether putting a roller coaster in the middle of Epcot will bring in more teenagers or just turn off our current guests.

Finally, if we know we're going to get a core audience of white middle class families from large metropolitan areas, we should spend some time figuring out how to increase our attendance by appealing to other groups, too. Disney World has a tremendous number of Canadian, English and Brazilian visitors. How does one resort (albeit one with multiple theme parks) appeal to this very diverse group?

It's easy to see that demographics will impact our designs in many ways. In future chapters, as we talk about types of attractions and how to collect them into a park, never lose sight of this core principle of theme park design: who are your guests?

Chapter 3: Up and Running

It takes people to run a theme park. Something like 100,000 at Walt Disney World alone. When we visit a park we see the costumed characters, the ticket takers, the kitchen workers, and maybe a few custodial people. But there are hundreds of people behind the scenes for every one we meet "on stage".

Who are all these people, and what do they do?

Operations

Operations personnel are the most visible people in the park. These are the people who interact with the guests the most, because they operate the rides. That can mean anything from taking tickets to driving a boat while delivering a comedy monologue on the Jungle Boat Cruise—that's how comedian Steve Martin got his start, by the way.

Many operations people are "casual temporaries" which in theme park parlance means "don't call us, we'll call you". But an equal number are full time employees, who after some experience become "leads" of attractions or perhaps whole lands. They in turn report to supervisors responsible for operation of the entire park.

Maintenance

There's a lot of stuff to break in a theme park. Everything that moves, everything that has electricity or water—but hopefully not both —flowing through it is liable to break at some point or other. It can take hundreds of maintenance people to properly maintain a large theme park. Some of these jobs are quite specialized: film projector maintenance, vehicle mechanic, computer control systems specialist, audio technician, even scuba divers to keep aquarium facilities maintained.

In some parks the custodial personnel also report to Maintenance, but in others it is a separate department.

Food Service

Fixing 20,000 hamburgers a day can be a challenge. (Fixing 20,000 edible ones can be an insurmountable challenge.) But not only do you need to fix them, you need to get the fresh, raw materials where they're needed when they're needed, which involves a whole set of logistics. That's what food service and its management does 365 days a year.

Food service is a significant contributor to the bottom line in theme park revenues. In some parks with fancy sit-down restaurants, food service revenues for some guests will exceed the front gate receipts. So food and food quality become more important at theme parks every year.

Recent trends have also shown that theme park guests will pay a little more to eat healthy food. Well, some of them, anyway. Legoland has been successful in offering fresh foods in a farmer's market-like environment to parents wanting a healthier choice than hamburgers and hotdogs.

Merchandising

This is the other major contributor to theme park revenues. There was a time when the souvenir shops were just near the park exits, but now they are everywhere, tied in with each area's theming. And the goal of many major new attractions is to provide a shop at exit where themed merchandise or photos taken on the ride are available. There's even a website called exitthroughretail.com! (I should know. It's mine.)

Anyway, someone has to think up all those T-shirt slogans, keep the warehouses filled with coffee mugs, and buy all that plastic cra—

Ahem. Well, you get the idea. There are lots of people in merchandising and its related logistics departments, and they represent a major profit center, often more than the front gate.

Management

These are the guys who run everything. At the level below president will be vice-presidents responsible for the aforementioned departments, plus a number of overhead departments including Finance, Planning and Marketing.

One of my friends runs a department devoted to figuring out how many guests will be in each park at a major Florida resort on every day for the next five years.

Think about that.

What factors could influence it? Day of week, school holidays, weather patterns (including the likelihood of tropical storms during a given week), the Super Bowl and other television or world events, not to mention whether we theme park engineers are designing them a new attraction for that season.

And why does anyone need to know this?

What if Mondays in winter have an average attendance of 15,000 people, and then 40,000 people show up at your park one Monday because it's a school holiday? You're gonna need a heap of burgers to satisfy that crowd. Plus more ride operators, food service personnel, cashiers, custodians, and on and on. Time to call the casual temporaries!

Clearly a theme park is a complex collection of inter-related disciplines, and there is a lot more going on behind the scenes than the average visitor would guess.

Chapter 4: What If We...?

Creative People

As much as I'd like you to believe that the world revolves around theme park engineers, new attractions don't start with us. They start with the Creative People.

That's not to say that theme park engineers aren't creative. It's just that the creative people *think* we aren't.

Getting a creative person to take a suggestion from an electronic engineer is like trying to feed squid to a baby. Well, maybe Japanese babies like squid, I don't know. Anyway, I wouldn't let one handle a soldering iron—the Creative Person or the baby—so I guess that's fair.

Creative People fall into several camps. There are art directors, the guys who wander around the park holding up paint samples and fabric swatches. Writers come up with the basic story line of an attraction, and polish the script as it develops. Set Designers perform the same function that they do in legitimate theater, designing sets, backgrounds and props for attractions. Media Designers produce the audio and video materials that will be played—over and over and over—in each attraction. Their job is similar to that of Filmmakers, although the latter have larger budgets. And there are hundreds of other professions that may also be involved in the conceptual phase of a new attraction: composers, actors, story board artists and so on.

Once they figure out—more or less—what they want to do, that's when the Technical People become involved. We figure out how much the whole thing will cost and then tell them they can't afford it.

The Creative People go off in a huff, change a bunch of stuff, then present their new ideas. About half the time the new way actually is cheaper than their first approach.

Anyway, you get the idea. There's a lot of give and take before the attraction's initial design is baselined, and even more as the details are firmed up, usually while we're trying to build it. Changes can make for an interesting time, all right.

Technical People

Who are the Technical People that are torturing these poor Creative People? They're us. Let's do a quick run down of the theme park engineering skills we'll be learning about during the rest of this book.

Show Control Engineers are at the eye of this storm. Call me prejudiced (since I am one) but Show Control is the most cross-disciplinary of all theme park engineering jobs. The show control engineer needs to know a little bit about every system that he or she connects with—ride, audio, video, lighting, mechanical, facility, safety —even wind monitors on occasion! And since the show control system is connected to virtually everything—including the things that go into the attraction at the last minute—the show control engineer is usually the person working at four o'clock in the morning on opening day trying to get things to work. This situation isn't helped by the fact that the show control engineer is responsible for controlling and synchronizing all of the audio and video media in the attraction, most of which isn't available until about 3:30 of that same day.

Ride Control engineers drink the most coffee. Whether this is why they all have that nervous tremor, I can't say. Anything big and moving fast is typically controlled by these guys. They understand redundant computing systems, fail safe design, single and multiple point failure analysis and a lot more. The show control and ride control systems cue each other for synchronization purposes, but they are nearly always independent systems.

Audio/Video Engineers design the systems that play, process, distribute and deliver the audio and video throughout an attraction. Notice that they don't design the media itself. This is done by producers, directors and recording artists. The audio/video engineers make sure that their material looks and sounds good, and works reliably for the attraction's designed lifespan. Typically the actual control of audio and video is done by the show control engineer.

Architects design the building itself, and Architectural Engineers make sure it will stand up. Given the fanciful structures of many themed attractions, this is no small feat. They are generally Structural or Civil Engineers.

Mechanical Engineers design nearly everything that moves: vehicles, set pieces, props, ride doors. They also work with hydraulics (oil or water) and pneumatics (air). Some smaller mechanical items may be handled by animators or special effects artists.

Systems Engineers unify all of these other disciplines. They often have oversight of the entire attraction's engineering, but are seldom intimately familiar with any single subsystem. The Systems Engineer is often the one who is ultimately responsible for ADA (Americans with Disabilities Act) compliance and meeting applicable safety codes.

Technical Writers document what we did. They write maintenance and operation manuals. A common problem with technical writers is that they may not fully understand what they are writing about. For this reason, there is a trend toward the design engineers preparing their own technical documentation.

Lighting Designers fall somewhere between the Creative People and the Technical People. The selection and location of fixtures and colored filters is certainly an artistic endeavor. But the selection of Dimmer Cabinets and control equipment is a technical one. Sometimes the show control engineer participates in the technical portion of this task. And we're always grateful when the lighting designer has an idea of the technical ramifications of his or her design.

Special Effects Designers also fall somewhere between the Creative People and the Technical People. They have long, scraggly beards, and walk around hunched over, like forest gnomes, muttering about smoke fluid and synthetic mud. And you should see their husbands. Special Effects people often design their own electronic control boxes to activate their effects. But not if the show control engineer can help it. These two disciplines have a long history of miscommunication. I think it has something to do with the smoke fluid.

Coordinators are like honey bees. They flit from discipline to discipline, collecting the needs of one and passing it on to the next. As opening day gets closer they flit faster and faster.

Planners and Schedulers use project timeline software and spreadsheets to put together highly detailed schedules that are read only by upper level management. The rest of us are just working as fast as we can and making up bogus percentages of completion to keep them happy.

Estimators and Financial Analysts are the people who figure out how much more the attraction is costing than it was supposed to, and then try to explain why.

Project Managers are the guys who think they're running the project, when really it is a three-ton bull escaped from its pen and bearing down on opening day no matter what happens. Along the way they organize lots of meetings where they try to encourage communication between the various engineering disciplines, construction personnel and Creative People. One of their vital functions is to bring lots of pizza in the middle of the night. In the end, if the show doesn't stink, they get the credit.

***

In these past few chapters we've talked about people. I've discussed three major groups.

Our guests are the people for whom we design the parks. We need to understand the demographics of our guests to make sure they're satisfied, and to try to figure out how to expand our attraction's appeal. It's clear there are a wide variety of possible dedicated venues, which may attract very diverse guests. Different attractions appeal to very different people, and we need to take that into account during our design work.

Operations people are, in a sense, our true customers. When we design a park, they are the ones who will take delivery, operate and maintain it. At every stage of design we should ask ourselves, "Does this work, is it operable, is it maintainable?"

Our compatriots are the creative and technical people with whom we partner to build a new attraction. We need to understand their needs and make our requirements known to them so that together we can achieve the optimum result: an attraction that will be the talk of the town, the buzz of the industry, and well one that will have very long lines. And not because it's broken half the time.

You've also learned a bit about me, and how I ended up as a theme park engineer by accident.

Next we'll talk about attractions, and why story is the single most important element. In the mean time don't forget: keep your hands and arms inside the vehicle at all times.

Chapter 5: Rides

Why Story is King

When people think of theme parks, the first thing they think of are attractions. Everyone has his or her favorites. When I was a kid it was a toss up whether my favorite was Disneyland's Pirates of the Caribbean or The Haunted Mansion. With delicious anticipation I'd stand in the queue line soaking up the set design and theming, getting completely immersed in the environment; I would soon eagerly board the ride and try to capture every detail as we rushed through and then, as soon as the ride was over, run around to the front of the building, get back in line and do it again. In retrospect, I now know the thing that made these my favorite attractions was the story they told. I've come to realize that story is the key ingredient in any great themed attraction. If we don't leave our guests with the memory of an emotional journey, we haven't really succeeded in taking them on the ride they paid for.

Even though I was a kid a pretty long time ago—let's just say that back then dinosaur rides involved the real thing—nearly all of the storytelling techniques found in today's theme parks had already been invented. What hadn't been invented are the technologies we use today to tell those stories. Simulators, digital video, wire-guided vehicles, even microcomputers themselves have all come along since I was a kid. It's impossible to imagine building any new attraction without using some —perhaps even all—of those technologies. Yet even as we do, we need to remember that story is still king.

Let's look at the different types of experiences available in today's theme parks, and try to understand how they transport us to another reality and keep us coming back.

Gravity and Iron Rides

For pure, pulse-quickening power, nothing can really match falling out of your mom's shopping cart. But for those of us too big to fit in that little fold-down seat anymore—and too chicken to take up skydiving or bungee jumping—there are gravity rides. These are the roller coasters, parachute drops, "Big Shots" and anything else that uses the principle that what goes up must come down. In the trade we call them "hard iron" rides because usually the track and its supports are welded steel. For the roller coaster purist, though, old-fashioned wooden scaffolding still holds a certain allure. But the advent of tubular steel rails—often pressurized and monitored to detect fractures —has enabled coasters to do things never imagined with wood: vertical loops, cork screws, and speeds approaching 100 miles per hour are features of some of today's favorite gravity rides.

Most gravity rides don't tell much of a story, and perhaps that's why I'm not a big fan. But they're a definite lure for a certain type of theme park guest, and some fairly unthemed theme parks have very little except gravity rides.

Dark Rides

Dark rides are, well, rides in the dark. They date back at least to the Coney Island era and the scandalous Tunnel of Love. But today we're likely to think of something a bit more family oriented when we talk about dark rides. The classic dark rides of the Disneyland era are those in Fantasyland: Peter Pan's Flight, Alice's Adventures in Wonderland, Snow White's Scary Adventure, and my favorite—and long gone—Mr. Toad's Wild Ride. One can also argue that some very high-tech modern rides such as Spiderman at Universal Studios Florida and Tower of Terror at Disney MGM Studios are simply elaborate dark rides, but I think that is selling them short. These are really hybrids, and will be discussed in a separate section.

After the initial construction of Fantasyland, Disney upped the ante for dark rides by introducing Pirates of the Caribbean and

Haunted Mansion. These two dark rides became the standard by which all others are still judged, because they had three dimensional animation, special effects, synchronized audio throughout the ride, and strong storylines.

For our purposes, dark rides are relatively small, low-throughput rides where individual vehicles—or sometimes strings of vehicles—move through sets and animation that is often illuminated chiefly by ultraviolet ("black") light, making the colors glow vividly. The vehicles may be suspended from overhead as in Peter Pan, or pulled by a chain drive as in Epcot's defunct World of Motion, or float, but usually they follow a single, wiggly rail, which may ascend—as in Alice and Wonderland—or simply wander all over hell's half acre, as in Mr. Toad, who literally found himself bedeviled in the end.

Boat Rides

It floats. It's a boat. What makes it a ride? Usually a track or a trough that guides the boat through scenery and animation. Some dark rides use boats as a conveyance mechanism, but most boat rides are outdoors. Boats can be small, such as in the Fantasyland boat ride, medium as on the Jungle Boat Cruise, or large as in the Mark Twain paddlewheeler (yes, it's on tracks). They can also sometimes be guest-piloted, notably the wilderness canoe ride. Nothing very high-tech there.

Simulators

This was the great technical breakthrough of the 1980s. Used for decades to train military and commercial airline pilots, simulators first made their way into the themed entertainment market at CN Tower in Toronto and, shortly after that, in Disney's collaboration with George Lucas, Star Tours. Simulators allow theme parks to take guests to places that could never be convincingly, well, simulated by other ride mechanisms.

Some simulators place the guests on a moving motion base in a large, open space. An example of this is Universal Studio's Back to the Future, where multiple motion bases operate beneath one of two IMAX dome theaters.

More convincing—to my mind—are simulators such as Star Tours and SeaWorld's Arctic Adventure where the guests are completely surrounded by the simulator, allowing no fixed external reference points. Of course, this also means that unless the simulation is nearly perfect, motion sickness is a real possibility. Body Wars at Epcot's Wonders of Life is a good example of this problem. The enclosed environment and rhythmic motion, coupled with discrepancies between the motion profile and the projected scenery make many guests physically ill.

One of the things that attracted theme parks to simulators was the ability to re-theme attractions without the capital investment of new props and animation. In point of fact, few theme park simulators have been re-themed, although some of the films have been freshened. It is debatable whether the cost of a new film and motion profile are justified by renewed guest interest, since only the most alert visitors are likely to detect the change of media in an otherwise unaltered building.

Lately simulators have become inexpensive enough to find their way into neighborhood malls and family entertainment centers. Because a neutrally themed simulator can offer a variety of completely different ride experiences, mall operators get the benefit of selling tickets for dozens of different rides while only needing a single investment in hardware. Ironically the flexibility of the simulator, which originally attracted the theme parks, now works against them, since once there is one in every mall, the simulator no longer carries the cachet that made it special in the theme park.

To counter this, theme parks have begun upping the ante, combining simulators with other technologies. The frontrunner in this endeavor is Universal Studios. Their Spiderman ride at Islands of Adventure is widely regarded as the world's greatest theme park attraction. It places an open top motion base on a ride vehicle and moves it through an extremely elaborate dark ride with 3-D projection in each scene. The 3-D animation is perfectly synchronized with the vehicle and motion base, allowing characters to jump from buildings, with their impact "felt" as they land on the vehicle. It's a truly amazing experience.

Virtual Reality

One step beyond simulators, virtual reality eliminates even the moving theater from the ride experience. Don the goggles, and the environment is delivered directly to your pupils. Disney's Research and Development created a sophisticated VR attraction for their Disney Quest family entertainment centers. Sitting on a bench and using handlebars to guide your motion, you fly your magic carpet though Aladdin's hometown.

Theme parks have struggled with virtual reality. It presents many challenges that make it a problem for their environment. Virtual reality is very low throughput. Because your trip through the alternate reality is generally self-directed, it tends to have a non-linear storyline, or perhaps even no story at all. There is also some evidence that a less than perfect VR experience can lead to alteration in the way the brain responds to visual motion input, after even short periods of exposure; this is a form of brain damage, and needs to be carefully considered before the further proliferation of this technology.

Finally, as personal computers become more powerful, they will be able to deliver a wealth of VR experiences at home. Current thinking is that VR represents competition to theme parks, not opportunity.

Carny Rides

Sometimes themeparks use rides found in carnivals and states fairs. These rides typically circle or spin, and occupy a relatively small footprint. Theming brings added value to an otherwise off-the-shelf product. The classic example is Disneyland's popular flying Dumbo ride. In a similar vein, the spinning teacups in Fantasyland are a modification of 1920s boardwalk rides. The new dinosaur land at

Disney's Animal Kingdom incorporates the latest of these vended rides. Called the "mouse" it is a roller coaster with vehicles that spin.

It's important when incorporating carny rides into a theme park that there be some "added value". Not just the paint job, but even the purpose of the ride must fit the theme of the area. Otherwise we lose the storyline. Knott's Berry Farm did a relatively poor job of this on their original Fiesta Village area, but additional landscaping, façade work and food service eventually turned the area into a truly Mexican themed land.

Other Rides

The imagination of theme park designers is nearly unlimited, and there are plenty of rides that don't fit into any of these categories. A plethora may be found at the Legoland parks in Denmark, England, California, Florida and Germany. Here is a quick sampling:

- Small electric cars that kids really drive themselves, on a grid of miniature city streets.
- A motor assisted rope pulley system that allows you to pull yourself and a friend to the top of a tall tower.
- Walk-throughs. These are some of my favorites. Build a ride, then leave out the vehicles. Let the guests walk through the scenes at their own pace. This is a fabulous, inexpensive way to tell a story.

Transportation Systems

How to get around the park? Or in some cases between parks. Trains, Boats and Monorails are themed attractions in themselves. They do the work of moving guests from one spot to another while entertaining them. Transportation systems have the additional challenge of having to fit in with the theme of every area they pass through, or they disrupt the storyline. That's why Disneyland's monorail couldn't stop in, say, Frontierland. But a train can stop almost anywhere.

Chapter 6: Shows

Most theme parks offer their guests a mix of ride and "sit down" shows. While rides are the main attraction for teenagers, theaters appeal to the younger and older demographic, and provide weary guests a place to rest their feet—or their stomachs.

It's much easier to tell a story in a theater. In fact it's hard NOT to tell a story in a theater. But in theme parks it's important that the theater itself—both inside and out—fit the theme.

There is a temptation, perhaps even a trend, to turn theaters into "black boxes" that can host a variety of shows because they have completely neutral theming. This is a bad idea. Guests are subliminally aware when the story doesn't permeate the entire experience, and this kind of venue tends to leave them feeling like they would have been smarter to just spend a few bucks at the neighborhood Cineplex.

Automated Theaters

Automated theaters represent about half of all theaters in theme park venues. While the film projection in even your neighborhood cinema is automated to some extent these days, when we talk about automated theaters we mean theaters where the entire show cycle is automated: entrance doors, exit doors, curtains (if any), lighting and so on.

The actual content of automated theaters varies widely, from a simple 35 mm or video projection to nine-screen 70 mm Circlevision, or to a theater with animated figures on a stage, such as Country Bear Jamboree.

One of the best fully automated theaters I've seen is at the Pro Football Hall of Fame in Canton, Ohio. It's the best because of an exceptionally strong storyline.

The show, designed by Edwards Technologies, puts guests in the role of pro football players going to the Super Bowl. Preshow monitors outside the theater let you experience the tailgate party craziness of the parking lot before the big game.

As you enter the theater you're really stepping into a vehicle: it's a rotating platform divided into two halves. In the first half a high-definition film takes you inside the locker room, where the coach is giving his players a pre-game pep talk.

At the end of his talk, the players head out into the corridor that leads to the field, and you begin to rotate 180 degrees. Abstract images of marching players and the echo of their footfalls in the corridors accompany the rotation. The space you arrive in is much larger than the first theater.

A tiny, lighted doorway appears far ahead, then swells in size to occupy a large screen projection as you burst onto the field. The crowd roars in bone-jarring surround sound. And the game begins. In close-up.

Each year NFL films produces a new film for this theater, with spectacular highlights from the most recent Super Bowl. This is a show where not only is story king, it's real.

Live Theaters

Live theater is the theme park attraction with the longest history, dating back to the Ancient Greeks, or possibly even to cave men wearing funny hats. Traditionally, live theater has been a very manual affair: a guy backstage pulls the levers that control the rigging, and a guy in the rafters works the spotlight. But in recent years, larger stage productions, especially Broadway shows and touring companies, have come to rely on show control systems to handle at least a portion of the cues. Complex lighting, moving set pieces and special effects all require some level of automation. But the performers still do it the old fashioned way, and the lighting and musical cues are still triggered by a guy—possibly wearing a funny hat—sitting out in the theater someplace.

In theme parks, live shows are likely to be more canned than that. Yes, there's a technical director working one or more "boards" in the audience, but much of the timing for lighting, staging and music is predetermined, and the performers voices may not even be live. In fact the only live thing about a heavily costumed stage show in a theme park may be the guys sweating inside those bulky costumes.

Hybrid Theaters

Hybrid theaters are mixtures of live performers and highly automated lighting and sets. The dividing line may be thin between these shows and fully automated or live theaters. To me, the distinction is this: if the show would be meaningless without both the live and automated elements combined perfectly, it's a hybrid theater.

A wonderful small hybrid theater is the Aegis show at Nauticus, the National Maritime Center in Norfolk, Virginia. Aegis is the Greek word for shield. It's also the name of the Navy's high-tech protection system used by AEGIS-class destroyers to form a 250-mile-radius shield around a naval battle group. The Aegis Theater combines video, lighting and effects to simulate a battle situation in the control room of such a ship. Live performers on stage play the role of crew members, and the audience uses voting consoles in the arm of the theater seats to determine the outcome of the show.

Another superb hybrid theater is Mystery Lodge at Knott's Berry Farm in Buena Park California. In this brilliant show designed by Bob Rogers, you are seated in a traditional long house and watch an old Indian summon visions from the fire, shaping the smoke into objects that illustrate his stories. The Indian is a live actor, and the smoke is well, magic. At the end of the show, the live performer evaporates before your eyes.

That's entertainment!

Stunt Theaters

Stunt theaters are special forms of hybrid theaters, where live actors not only mix with highly automated props, but do so in potentially dangerous ways. Special life safety issues must be taken into account when dealing with exploding gas, dangerous set piece movements and pyrotechnics.

Chapter 7: Other Attractions

A full-scale theme park has plenty of things other than major rides and shows. In fact it's mainly this stuff that makes it a "themed" park. What would Adventureland be without a jungle? Or Frontierland without a fort? The landscaping, facades, paving, even the trash receptacles all contribute to the theming. Most of this stuff isn't very interactive, though, although I have seen talking robotic trash cans.

Here are some of the other themed attractions you'll find in many parks.

Arcades

Arcades are the black hole of theme parks, sucking in endless streams of quarters. They cater to the teenage demographic, and have an extremely low initial cost and almost no operating cost.

The challenge with arcades is to maintain any kind of theming. There are plenty of arcades in neighborhood malls. Finding one in a theme park sometimes seems, well, cheap. To keep the experience special, a smart themed attraction selects games (or custom designs them) to fit into the overall theme, and then adds heavy set decoration to the entire gaming area.

The most successful example of this I've seen is the area outside Star Trek The Experience at the Las Vegas Hilton. It's really a casino, not an arcade, but the only difference is that in a casino you pretend you're not going to lose all your quarters until it actually happens. Everything in the Star Trek Experience casino looks like it came straight off the Enterprise: chrome and black slot machines, barstools, and railings, high-tech wall panels, even overhead laser beams.

It's so good it makes your pockets itch.

Interactives

Interactive share the theming problem with arcades. An interactive device plopped into the middle of a museum doesn't enhance the venue unless it is completely custom designed—including the console —to specifically fit into the theme. If it's just a computer in a box it may as well be mailed to you on a CD-ROM.

One of the first really successful interactives was SMART-1, a voice activated robot in Epcot's Communicore. SMART-1 could move, carry on a conversation and play games with ANYONE, responding to "yes", "no" and a few other words. This was a pretty impressive speech recognition feat in 1982.

The best interactive I've seen is the Land the Shuttle simulator at NASA's Space Center Houston. We've all seen flight simulators run on $400 PCs. What Land the Shuttle brings to the game is multiple screens filled with authentic dials and readouts that accurately reproduce the shuttle's control surfaces, and a personal flight instructor named Chet who interacts with you as you try to land that flying brick on an itty-bitty runway. Chet actually walks around among the controls at one point, and appears outside the front window wearing an automobile steering wheel around his neck after particularly rough landings. The media, designed by BRC Imagination Arts, has the player and spectators in stitches from opening until closing every day. And it tells a story.

Exhibits

An exhibit that adequately matches the attraction theming can be just as effective as much more expensive alternatives. As some one who makes his living selling sophisticated control, audio and video equipment I probably shouldn't admit that well-themed static exhibits are among my favorite attractions. But they are.

An excellent example is the Tutankhamen's Tomb at Busch Gardens Florida. It completes the theming of their Montu roller coaster area, but I'd much rather walk through the tomb than throw up on the coaster. Call me silly. Static lighting and continuous run audio impart a suitable spooky atmosphere to a fairly accurate reproduction of the contents of the famous king's burial chamber. Aside from a short introductory video there is no show. But it works. It tells a story.

Another exhibit area that works is the museum in the China pavilion at Epcot. Currently filled with elaborate animated clocks and other timepieces from the period when China was first coming into contact with the Western World, it perfectly complements the China Circlevision film and other themed areas of the attraction.

Food Service

While I find food fascinating, not everyone shares my enthusiasm. So theme parks need to go out of their way to make food entertaining. This means either theming the food service, theming the food itself, or both.

Sometimes all that means is the right building. You wouldn't buy a hotdog in Tomorrowland if they served it from a plywood hotdog stand. But put it in a chrome flying saucer and call it a Moondog and you can get six bucks for it.

Epcot's World Showcase is the ultimate in food theming. A continuous international expo where the countries of the world stand side by side, each pavilion serves its indigenous food in appropriate surroundings: Tatami Rooms in Japan, a bistro in France, and a plastics factory in England (just kidding). In 1983 we went on the same tour of Morocco that Disney's Art Directors took. Disney is particularly attentive to this theming. A few years later when the Morocco pavilion opened we found ourselves dining in a virtual copy of our hotel dining room in Rabat, right down to the inlaid tile patterns on the walls.

There's no question that this theming affects food sales. Many years ago when they installed turn-of-the-century popcorn wagons at Disneyland, things really started popping.

The potential of theming on sales was not lost on the food service industry as a whole. Chuck E. Cheese's Pizza Time Theater was the first to pioneer the highly themed restaurant. It featured a somewhat animated band of animals playing musical instrument and singing to entertain the kids while the pizza cooked. The pizza was actually pretty decent. Recent stores have been more modestly themed. The new plan focuses on more play areas and games for the kids, with the theming somewhat reduced.

Perhaps this is a reaction to the spread of theming to seemingly every neighborhood mall store and restaurant. It becomes increasingly difficult to distinguish yourself. Worst of all, pointless theming doesn't tell a story. It's just well, theming.

Other heavily themed restaurant chains include The Rainforest Café and Planet Hollywood. But the most successful is the Hard Rock Café, which has created a worldwide franchise by successfully combining music, food and rock 'n roll memorabilia. Now expanded into hotels and casinos, and things even came full circle when their name was licensed for a short-lived theme park!

Merchandising

Just as the right building can help you sell food, it can also help you sell merchandise. Often the two occupy the same building, and the merchandise is sold after dinner—or after the show or ride—as you "Exit Through Retail".

Appropriate selection of merchandise is critical in a truly themed environment. While you might be able to get away with T-shirts almost anywhere, you cannot sell lava lamps in a medieval castle.

***

In the last few chapters we've talked about why the best theme park attractions are built around a strong storyline. Story is, indeed, king. Whether you're building a ride, a show, or some other attraction it will only be truly effective in a themed environment if it moves us not just physically, but also emotionally.

We've surveyed the broad range of ride technologies available to theme parks, from roller coasters to boat rides, and the latest high-tech simulators. We've also talked about the range of theatrical experiences, from fully automated Circlevision theaters to live stage or stunt shows. And finally we looked at ways to incorporate other elements into a themed experience, including making food service and merchandise shopping fun for guests with money still left in their wallets after passing through the front gate.

Next we'll begin planning our first attraction. We'll start with the Blue Sky phase of brainstorming ideas until we've settled on a storyline. Then, by determining the target audience, we'll pick a ride or show technology that suits it. And finally we'll try to anticipate the real-world constraints that may affect us once we begin the technical design of our attraction.

Until then, please remain behind the yellow line until the doors open.

Chapter 8: Concept

Let's begin with the early stages of design, from Blue Sky through initial story creation, then the process of fitting the story to our intended audience and finally trying to figure out whether it fits within the real world's design constraints.

The design of every theme park attraction begins with a blue-sky phase. This is where the Creative Team sits around a large table and brainstorms new ideas for the attraction. It usually goes something like this:

"Wait, wait, I know! We can have these lily pads floating above the surface of the lake—there'll be a railing around the edge of them, of course. People will stand on the lily pads and aim lasers, trying to knock each other into the water."

"Won't that be dangerous?"

"No, the engineers will figure out a way to make the lasers safe."

"How will the lily pads float?"

"Oh, the engineers will come up with something."

You get the idea. Most attractions start out with a completely impossible idea, either because it can't be done or can't be done at a reasonable cost. So the design of attractions ends up being a negotiation process between the Creative Team, the Engineers, and the Estimators who are caught in the middle.

Eventually they will all agree on a design that is achievable at a price within the budget. At least, they think they have agreed. Then the engineers go off and design something that is nothing like the Creative Teams imagined. At the same time the Creative Team starts trying to slip back in all the impossible stuff that they previously agreed to take out. And the estimators keep telling both groups not to spend any more money.

It's an iterative process.

Eventually time, money, patience or all three runs out and the attraction opens to the public. Then the Creative Team studies the public's reaction to their creation and come up with a whole bunch of new ideas for improvements. The engineers now change to the graveyard shift, and try to figure out how to shoehorn in all this new stuff, without exceeding the original budget and without impacting the next day's operation of the attraction.

As you can see, the blue-sky process never really stops.

Walt Disney once said that as long as there was imagination in the hearts of men, Disneyland would never be finished. I'm not sure whether the irony was intended.

Chapter 9: Why Story Is King

What was wrong with my lily pad attraction?

It had no story. If story is king, then even at the beginning of blue sky there must be story.

If the evil goblins have besieged the city and the fairy people have taken flight on floating lily pads, trying to defend themselves using anti-goblin guns, then we have the story. We can worry about the antigravity part later.

Why is this concept so much more involving than my original description?

It's because we immediately sense that there is an objective here: two sides—right and wrong—and a battle to be fought. We subliminally align ourselves with one of those sides—probably the fairy people, although certain segment of our target market may be more inclined to play the goblin role.

Let's take an example. A roller coaster careens through a darkened room over a faintly illuminated cityscape. Enthralling? Not really, there's no story.

Take two. A rock band is late for a concert at the Hollywood Bowl. They invite you to hop in their limo and go careening through the Hollywood Hills and all around the L.A. freeway system to make it on time. That's the story behind Disney MGM's Rock 'n Roller coaster, and it works.

How about this one: you climb aboard a BART subway train. It pulls out of the station, then begins to shake as an earthquake strikes. Fires erupt, and a flood comes cascading down the tunnel, extinguishing the flames and splashing over the train. Exciting? I guess. But not completely fulfilling. Why? They forgot to tell us why we were getting on the train, where it was going, and what our mission was. The name of this attraction at Universal Studios Florida is Earthquake, so we knew what to expect when we got on. But there was no underlying story to get us involved.

Here are two more real ones, one that doesn't work, one that does:

A boat glides through a dark tunnel. It passes a volcano, people at a bazaar trying to sell us things, Mayan ruins, dancing dolls with colorful costumes, and fiber-optic fireworks.

A boat glides through a dark tunnel. It passes a ship full of pirates and a fort. A battle is underway. Cannon balls whiz overhead, and explosions dot the water. Farther along the pirates have seized the village and are auctioning off the women, stealing treasures, and setting fire to the buildings. As we barely escape from the burning timbers we see prisoners still trapped in the jail, trying to lure a dog into bringing them the keys to their cell.

Which ride has a story, the Mexico pavilion at Epcot or Pirates of the Caribbean?

It's not that hard from the outset to make sure that a ride has a story, which makes it surprising that so many rides don't have one. But a lot of them don't. I'm not talking about rides in amusement parks. I'm talking about rides in theme parks. In amusement parks when we see an iron roller coaster we expect to be tossed around a little; we don't expect a story. That's why it's called an amusement park, not a theme park. But at a theme park our expectations are higher. Do the Batman or Superman roller coasters at Six Flags theme parks tell a story, or are there simply themed façades accompanying an unthemed ride?

Sometimes there might be a story there, but it isn't intelligibly conveyed to the riders. At the Journey to Atlantis flume ride at SeaWorld Orlando, preshow monitors show news broadcasts and interviews related to the reappearance of the lost continent of Atlantis. A Greek fishermen is involved, and a statue of the sea horse. The audio is usually intelligible, but the set up doesn't ever give us a mission. Once on the ride the audio becomes unintelligible, and animated figures and props—presumably there to convey a story—pass by so quickly that they can't be perceived. There's some kind of woman or witch in a very bad mood, and a reappearance of the sea horse. Then we go down a really nice drop, get soaking wet, creep back an upramp, and get one final surprise before unloading. It's not a bad ride, but it's incomprehensible.

Sometimes the story is just too complicated for the ride. The Lord of the Rings makes a great book and movie trilogy, but would it make a good ride? Of course not. Rides with more complicated storylines are often best implemented using simulators. Here it is customary to have a narrator—often the driver—who can summarize the adventure as it proceeds. And since simulator rides can be as long as ten minutes, there's more opportunity to convey the story.

Conversely, short rides need simple plots. You step into a basket, are hauled to the top of a tower, and dropped. Or... you go to a creepy old hotel where guests mysteriously vanished in an elevator years before... as you enter the darkened elevator shaft you suddenly feel yourself falling. Knott's Berry Farm's Parachute Drop or Disney MGM's Tower of Terror: which is the better ride? Tower of Terror. Of course, it cost 50 times more.

The year after Tower of Terror opened, it was updated and re-advertised as Tower of Terror 2. The new version dropped guests twice.

The next year they added even more drops, and then more. So now that Tower of Terror drops you four or five times for no particular reason, is it a better ride? That's a tough call. It's more exciting, however the story suffers. But it does allow the marketing folks to advertise the new ride profile each year.

A particularly effective mechanism for storytelling is the old-fashioned dark ride. Here a simple vehicle moves along a track—sometimes level sometimes with elevation changes—traveling from scene to scene and telling a linear story. The dark interior allows ultraviolet lighting to focus your guests' attention on the elements most important to the story. Still, one needs to be careful not to try to tell too complex a story. We all know the story of Alice in Wonderland. Without that background the ride at Disneyland would be nearly incomprehensible. But because of that shared background, the audience can relive the book or Disney movie without confusion. This foreknowledge of your guests' background is essential to a successful ride.

Chapter 10: Fitting Story to Audience

My grandmother never rode a roller coaster. And punk rockers don't hang out in butterfly conservatories.

It's essential to know your audience when designing an attraction. This process of evaluating the audience begins almost from the first moment of blue-sky and doesn't end until the concept moves from Art Direction to Engineering. Even then the mechanical or ergonomic design of the attraction may be influenced by its anticipated guests. For example, in Europe it's okay to make guests climb stairs or jump off of slowly moving vehicles. In America it's not. Let's look at how the designers of some other attractions targeted their audiences in order to see how we should proceed.

When the Las Vegas Hilton decided to install the Star Trek experience, they made a calculated decision to recreate the Starship Enterprise from the television series Star Trek: The Next Generation. They didn't use starships from the classic series of the late '60s or from more recent sequels, such as Star Trek Voyager. Why did they make this calculated decision?

It's because they knew their audience. The majority of people likely to visit the Star Trek Experience (and then spend time at the slot machines in the adjacent casino) are from an age group that would've watched Next Generation on television, but perhaps not the classic television show (except maybe in reruns).

When Legoland built their theme park in Carlsbad California they wanted an attraction where kids would be able to drive cars. There are lots of motorized go-cart racing places around the country, but they appeal more to teenagers than to Lego's target audience of preteens. Also, Lego didn't want anything so environmentally unfriendly and noisy. They wanted something more in keeping with the theme of their park: the Lego brand. So they decided to use electric cars.

The problem with electric cars is that they don't accelerate very quickly or go very fast. In a world where every third television show ends with a car chase, electric cars are about as exciting as watching fingerpaint dry. Lego had to figure out how to make electric cars interesting to kids. The solution is in the story. Lego created a kid-size grid of streets, laid out like the intersections in a real city, complete with stop signs and traffic lights. The idea was for kids to drive around the miniature city, following the same traffic laws that their parents have to follow. Clearly this was something that would appeal to the imagination of an 8-year-old if—and it's a big if—you can get him to do it.

To accomplish this they had to figure out a way to complete the story. The solution was to start the experience off with an instructional video that would teach kids how to observe the rules of the road: obey the signs and lights, use hand signals when turning, and be courteous to other drivers.

Another problem was getting kids to leave the vehicles once their time was up. They found the perfect solution in the completion of the story. At the exit of the attraction the kids are awarded Lego driving licenses.

The result: a simple ride becomes a complete experience though the use of story. A story designed specifically to appeal to the target audience: preteens.

Lets try using this awareness of our audience. In this week's assignment we're each going to put on our creative hat (the one with the bells and the moose antlers on it) and begin the design of our own themed attraction. It's a great way to really understand the blue sky-process.

Since an example is always worth a thousand words, I'll go first.

The best attractions reflect their creator's passion. I love history, so my attraction will be about history. There are so many regions and periods to choose from, it's hard to decide which to pick. I'm going to choose the Middle Ages—sometimes called the Dark Ages—because I think they have a lot of potential for entertainment and many people don't know much about them. The Middle Ages offer castles, knights, pageantry, eating with your fingers, the Black Plague and a total lack of sanitation. Some of these might not be the best ingredients for a themed attraction, but we can work around them.

My attraction needs a story. But where to start? The logical places to try to explain to my guests why they're in the Middle Ages. Better yet, perhaps we can make their getting to the Middle Ages a part of the attractions experience. Time travel. I like it. It mixes high-tech sci-fi with the history. There's potential here.

What if we created a way to convince guests that they were being transported into the past, and we made it so convincing that they couldn't figure out how we did it? Then, once we get them to the past, we give them an environment to play and: food, drink, entertainment, and something more. Let's make part of our story their quest to find a way back to the present.

Now let's consider our audience:

Families? Definitely.

Retired couples? Possibly.

International vacationers? If we put it someplace they visit.

Businessmen? Nope. Even if we're in a major convention city they're probably going to find something more um, stimulating to do with their time.

Teens on a date? Not likely.

OK, so we've got a tame crowd that may have trouble with physically demanding tasks or terrain, and that isn't in a hurry. So I'm picturing a medieval village with shops selling wooden toys, silk pennants, kites, lutes and fake swords. There are tents on a lawn where you can buy a turkey leg or a meat pie. We'll serve ale and soft drinks in pewter tankards. Street performers including jugglers or jesters will accost the guests, and generally try to liven things up.

You enter this land by some magical means that will transport you there instantly, and you'll have to discover the way back yourself.

That's enough to get started. The engineers will figure out the rest later. Let's do lunch.

Chapter 11: A Dose of Reality

Get ready for a hard dose of reality, Theme Park Engineers.

Art Direction just handed us a ten ton story idea and it's heading for a brick wall at a hundred miles per hour.

"'You enter this land by some magical means that will transport you there instantly'?" we say, as Engineers. "Come on, guys! Get real."

"No, no! That's the whole point of the concept," replies Art Direction. "We really need that to make the story work. We want them to start out in a library. A host will do a spiel. Then he'll pick up a big leather bund book, and when he opens it—poof! They're in the Middle Ages."

We engineers sigh, take our meeting notes and go back to our cubicles to scratch our heads.

I suppose it could be worse. They could want us to go down a whirlpool. Or be carried off in a tornado. Or plummet down an elevator shaft. Oh. Wait. We can do those.

Some of the best amusement rides started out as impossible ideas. As engineers we were called in to help design the control system for the vehicles on the Spiderman ride at Islands of Adventure. Here's the challenge we were facing:

The vehicle moves though eleven scenes, as the onboard motion base pitches and rolls the cabin. Both the vehicle's and the cabin's motion must be precisely synchronized with two off-vehicle 35 mm projectors that provide a 3D image. The film combines a portion of the cityscape background with animated characters who appear to swing through the air and even jump on your vehicle.

Synchronization is essential. When Spiderman lands on the front of your vehicle, you must feel the impact. And because your perspective changes as you move through the scene, building in the distance must change size at you approach them, and change perspective as you rotate.

Film projectors can't start on a dime. It takes them many seconds to get up to speed. And if 3-D films are even one frame (a tiny fraction of a second) off, the effect is ruined. The normal solution is to get them rolling, then synchronize everything else to them. But because it may take longer to load guests into a vehicle than we expect, we can never be sure when the vehicle will reach a given scene. So we have to stop and start the projectors.

Vehicles are mechanical. They don't always go at the speed we command, so we have to speed them up or slow them down to get to the right spot at the right time. But that will affect their synchronization along the way.

Clearly the whole thing is impossible. We even said that while we were working on it. The synchronization would never be good enough to be convincing.

Today it's operating as the world's greatest amusement ride.

Okay. So the engineers aren't always right.

But there are lots of things that can doom a themed attraction. Here are some of the real world constraints that the engineers face:

Practicality

Just because it's possible doesn't mean it's practical. We can send a man to the moon, but not an audience. At the circus they shoot people out of a cannon, but the average guest wouldn't enjoy it. And while I might enjoy an hour lecture about Estonian history, most guests would pay double just to get out.

We also can't afford anything that takes a long time to set up. Physically demanding attractions are pretty much out, as they greatly limit your audience. Dangerous attractions—like walking through a cave filled with recently fed lions—aren't a good idea. And attractions with slow logistics should be avoided—for example, loading guests onto tiny individual rafts and having them pole it across a river isn't very practical.

Maintainability

There's no point in building an attraction if we can't keep it operating. Nearly all rides and automated theaters involve mechanical equipment. This is usually were the trouble starts. It's relatively easy to design mechanisms that can perform a function once. It's much harder to design a mechanism that can repeat that same function hour after hour, day after day. And theme park mechanical systems take a lot of abuse, so the have to be sturdy.

One of the most fun rides ever was the Flying Saucers at Disneyland. One or two guests would board each of a couple dozen small flying saucers. They looked something like yellow inner tubes. The saucers sat on a large blue surface covered with tiny round flaps. When the ride was started the surface was pressurized with air. The blue flaps held the air in until a flying saucer moved over them. Then fingers on the bottom of the saucer pressed the flaps open, allowing the air to lift the saucer off the ground a few inches. By leaning one direction or another you could cause your saucer to glide around the ride area, bumping into other saucers, rebounding, or just speeding from one side to the other.

It was great fun.

It was also a maintenance nightmare.

There were tens of thousands of those little flaps. If only a few got stuck open there wasn't enough air to hold the saucers up. And they were incredibly difficult to fix.

In a couple of years the ride was gone, replaced by something more reliable.

Computers present a particular challenge for theme parks. While electronics are one of the most reliable components of a park, the mechanical systems that interact with them are notoriously problematical. You can rule out mice and keyboards right from the start. A theme park audience can destroy them in a day. But even some of the alternatives can be trouble.

At Space Center Houston we installed 24 interactive games about space. For example, one was called Orbital Rendezvous. It allowed you to experiment with the space shuttle's rocket engines, to see how orbital velocity affected orbital distance rather than speed. The goal was to dock with a space station.

The interface mechanism for Orbital Rendezvous was a touch screen. These have the advantage of no moving parts. There are many different touch screen technologies that work fine in an office environment. But in a theme park, touch screens take a severe beating. Only the optical break beam ones completely avoid wear and tear. These weren't that kind. With school kids jabbing their fingers at them all day long they lasted less than a month. At over a thousand US dollars each, it was a good thing that the sponsor of this attraction was also providing us with free touch screens.

Budget

Unlike those touch screens, most things aren't free. As theme park engineers we constantly face design, installation and maintenance budget constraints. There is a trade-off between the cost of choosing a technology that won't break and the cost of repairing a technology that will. Most engineers—and certainly all maintenance people—would prefer us to choose the former. But in the real world we often and up designing attractions to fit within the installation budget. The maintenance budget comes out of a completely different pocket.

Worse yet, it's easy for Art Direction to conceive of an attraction that we simply can't afford to build, no matter what technology we use.

I'm thinking our "instantaneous transportation back to medieval times" may fall into this category. Has anybody got any bright ideas yet?

Throughput

Just because we can build an attraction doesn't mean that we should. What if not enough people could enjoy an attraction to justify its expense? Virtual reality is notorious for having this problem. At Disney Quest the magic carpet simulator ride allows you to don a headset, on a control seat, and fly around Aladdin's home town. It's an amazing experience. But each simulator accommodates only one guest for about five minutes. Even with several simulators, only a few hundred guests get to try it each day. That's not practical in a theme park that can accommodate 50,000 people. Yet its development cost doesn't justify its use in a low throughput venue such as Disney Quest.

Safety

Some ride concepts are just too dangerous. One way of getting our guests instantaneously transported back to medieval times would be to drop them through a trap door. But even on a theater stage, with trained professionals who are expecting a trap door to open, performers are often hurt.

While state and federal regulation of thrill ride safety has been increasing, the safety of roller coasters and other thrill rides has historically been pretty good. You've got a lot higher chance of being injured in a traffic accident on the way to the theme park than you do while you're in the theme park.

Most theme park injuries occur not on thrill rides, but in more mundane ways. Leaving children untended to crawl out of vehicles or fall into water are two of the biggest causes of injury and death.

As theme park engineers we constantly need to keep in mind all factors that could affect the safety of a ride. And if the fundamental concept of the ride itself is unsafe, it is our responsibility to point that out.

ADA

Remember when you had to step off the curb at an intersection? Now nearly every intersection in the country has a wheelchair ramp each corner. This is the result of the Americans with Disabilities Act or ADA. The legislation mandated a broad range of accommodations for people with mobility, vision, and hearing disabilities.

This law also applies to theme parks. It has had a major impact on the design of theme park attractions—and their cost. Now theaters must provide captioning for the hearing-impaired, some signage must be presented in Braille, and most attractions must accommodate people in wheelchairs.

While no one has yet been forced to accommodate wheelchairs on a roller coaster, it's impossible to overstate the affect the ADA has had on the themed entertainment industry. We need to evaluate every attraction for compliance with this law.

Chapter 12: A Brainstorm

One of the neatest effects I've ever seen in a themed attraction was at the Star Trek Experience in the Las Vegas Hilton. After the queue area you stepped into a preshow room where there was a short presentation on overhead monitors. Suddenly the lights went off, there was a bright flash, and you were magically transported onto the Starship Enterprise. You found yourself standing in the Enterprise's transporter room, where a crew member briefed you on the story you had found yourself in.

It was magical.

Hey! That's it! That's how we'll get our guests back to medieval times. We'll steal—er, I mean emulate—the technique used at the Star Trek Experience.

So how did that effect work? There's really only one way that it could work. If you start out in one room, and in an impossibly short period of time find yourself in another larger room, they must have done the seemingly impossible. They pulled away the walls and the ceiling of the first room during the few moments you were in the dark. (Another clever element of this effect was that, once the doors closed, the room slowly and imperceptibly rotated, so that later, when you exited, it seemed as if you were walking through an area that should have overlapped with the entry. Quite mind-bending, really.)

Anyway, back to our attraction.

We'll start guests out in the library, and when our actor opens the book, we'll plunge them into darkness just long enough to pull away the set walls and ceiling. When the lights come on, they'll find themselves in a medieval castle.

I wonder if those Creative guys will buy me lunch?

***

In the past few chapters we looked at the early stages of design, from Blue Sky through initial story creation, then the process of fitting the story to our intended audience and finally trying to figure out whether it fits within the real world's design constraints.

I hope this process has gotten you so excited that attraction ideas are bouncing around in your head like ping pong balls at a bingo fundraiser.

Next we'll introduce your creative team and get down to the actual nuts and bolts of creative design.

Until then, please take small children by the hand and watch your step.

Chapter 13: Directors and Producers

Let's move forward in time to the next step after an attraction concept is approved. It's the last completely right-brain stage in the process, before the whole can of worms gets dumped into the engineers' cubicles and we start picking them out of our keyboards. To the engineers, that's when the real process of Theme Park Design begins. It helps us to understand what the creative team is trying to accomplish because it will impact the technical choices we make later. To strain a metaphor: we need to know whether the creative team intended to plant a garden or just go fishing.

While we were building Epcot we would often see its two main Art Directors, John Hench and Marty Sklar, walking around the partially constructed park. John would invariably be holding a handful of color swatches and Marty would be talking excitedly about the park. All of John's color swatches seemed to be pink or purple, and I sometimes wondered if anyone but him could really see the difference between the dozens of different shades. But he knew what he wanted, and he got it.

In addition to John and Marty, there were also Art Directors for each Epcot pavilion. Some of them, like Ward Kimball who did World of Motion, had been friends of Walt Disney's, and had made Disney movies before they got involved with theme parks. Others had grown up with theme parks.

Although they took completely different approaches, and used different story telling and visual techniques to tell their stories, each had a clear concept of how they wanted the attraction to turn out, and they worked throughout the project to keep the end result as close to that concept as possible.

In film production, the Art Director is the person who is responsible for the selection of colors, fabric and is responsible for the overall look of the movie. In theme parks their role may be far greater. Because of this, there is an increasing trend to call these people Show Producers. Sometimes the Show Producer will have an Art Director working for him or her, other times they will fill that role themselves. If the attraction incorporates a film, they are often the film Director, too. The Show Producer is ultimately responsible for the content of the entire attraction.

One of the best Art Directors in the business is Bob Rogers. Bob is an Academy Award nominated Director who worked with Disney on Epcot, Expo '86, and Space Center Houston. Bob's company, BRC Imagination Arts, has a long-standing relationship with General Motors. Bob designed both generations of postshow theaters at Epcot's General Motors pavilion, and designed the brilliant Mystery Lodge show for the GM sponsored pavilion at Expo '86.

Bob's most memorable attraction from Epcot days was The Bird And The Robot. In this lighthearted introduction to automation, an audio animatronic parrot—smoking a cigar—bosses around a cooperative robotic arm. The contrast between the artistry of the animatronic and the industry of the robot fascinated guests, and did a highly effective job of presenting General Motors' corporate message about the sophistication of their assembly lines. Bob credits Marty Sklar with the original idea for this attraction. Whoever thought of it, the implementation was brilliant. It was one of the most popular shows at Epcot before succumbing to a burst of spring-cleaning in the late '90s.

Although his title on The Bird And The Robot show was probably Art Director, Bob's role was really more like a Show Producer. Good Show Producers are hard to find. They must balance the needs of all the different people working on a project—both creative and technical —while keeping track of money and schedule. Show Producers spend a lot of time arbitrating disputes. They also become easy scapegoats when things go wrong. And they are always aware of problems in making if the team members aren't honest with them. It's a tough job.

Chapter 14: Writers

In 1982 construction began on a theme park between Walt Disney World and the neighboring town of Kissimmee. It was to be called "Little England" and would feature a medieval village where guests would participate in a Renaissance fair, complete with bawdy revelry, buxom serving girls proffering tankards of beer, and lots of eating with your fingers. After only a few months construction stopped. Today it's part of a housing development.

What went wrong?

It was the classic problem of story and audience. What was the story supposed to be? Why were we sweltering in the summer heat of Central Florida while pretending to be in a medieval village? And who was supposed to come to this theme park? A sizable percentage of the tourists who visit Walt Disney World are from England. Did anyone really think that these visitors would be interested in flying to Florida so that they could pay to get into a recreation of... England?! And nearly all visitors to Central Florida are families. Would they be interested in a "bawdy" experience?

Obviously, the answer was no.

That's where writers come in. If our writers do their job there'll be a reason for people to visit our medieval attraction. And the activities there will be appropriate to our audience.

When I think of writers I imagine an unshaven recluse, working in a lonely garret, cigarette dangling from one lip as he pounds out page after page of torrid text. Theme park writers aren't like that. They spend most of their time working with other members of the creative team. Most other time is spent developing refining ideas with these other people, in meetings and informal discussion groups.

But there is one way that theme park writers are just like my imaginary writer. They emphasize "backstory". Backstory is a term writers use to describe what happened before the beginning of the story. Backstory increases the believability of fiction because it guarantees each thing that happens in a novel has an underlying reason, even if we don't see it first-hand. For the same reason, backstory greatly increases the believability of a theme park attraction. If every themed item we encounter has an explanation for its existence —rather than just being empty set decoration—it will lend an aura of credibility to the attraction that the guests will perceive.

A terrific example of this is the Adventurers' Club at Pleasure Island in Disney World. The Art Director spent months traveling around the U.S. visiting flea markets and swap meets, collecting oddities from the past. The walls and ceiling of the entire attraction are peppered with these items.

But this is no neighborhood restaurant with knick knacks nailed to the walls. The writers worked out the backstory for hundreds of these objects. Small signs on many of them identify the (fictional) club member who procured the item, along with the time, place and circumstance of its acquisition.

They also created a club motto, and even a club song that visitors must learn. Costumed performers portraying club members wander through the space, interacting with visitors. They're not just reciting memorized acts. They're constantly ad-libbing while remaining in character. For these roles to work, the performer must be familiar with the entire backstory of his character. Portions of this backstory are played out, but others are never explicitly stated. Yet their existence lends credence to the whole.

Backstory can also backfire. The entire Pleasure Island complex is a good example. Each building had its own elaborate backstory— something about Merriweather Pleasure creating the place, and Fireworks blowing up one building, and they managed to work in a roller skating rink and a disco. Even reading the sheaf of explanatory papers they handed out to Operations on opening day was mind-boggling. The little brass plaques in front of each building were incomprehensible. How to convey the story to uninitiated tourists?

The answer is, they couldn't. It wasn't particularly well attended, and some of the venues were downright unpleasant. Operations took ownership, and over the course of a year added "streetmosphere"— stuff happening outside to give the place some character—in the form of redemption games, a live stage, and a DJ. Inside they re-themed several of the clubs and restaurants, converting a mall-like food court to a jazz club and the roller rink to a beach resort. (I hope the flooring contractor wasn't around the day they dumped sand all over his hardwood roller rink.)

Today, Pleasure Island has no story. A conscious decision was made to abandon it entirely. But as a collection of unrelated clubs it is now packed almost every night. And the bottom line is well, the bottom line.

Chapter 15: Artists

Curving up the steep, dark ascent into Spaceship Earth at Epcot has always filled me with anticipation. To the accompaniment of the eerie background music we hear the narrator—originally Walter Cronkite—chart our course through the history of communication. Even the creaking and moaning of the ride vehicles as they struggle up the hill creates a sense of something significant about to happen.

Ultimately cresting the top, we burst into a star field dome, with planet Earth floating above us. But for me, the best parts of the ride are the scenes of humans communicating, from the dawn of time onward: a chariot careens down a Roman street; giant printing presses churn out the Evening Herald; a newsboy hawks papers on the corner; telephone operators work at old-fashioned switchboards; and a girl in pajamas watches an early television set with her parents.

In each of these scenes the focus of our attention is on a central character—usually animated, although sometimes projected. But the sense of place and the emotion of the setting is created by the scenic and lighting design. Wood, metal, cloth and paint are squeezed through the Set Designer's telescope of forced perspective to create a believable, encompassing, and involving setting. Campfires crackle, gaslights glow, and television tubes flicker at the behest of the lighting designer. At their best, nothing can approach the quality of scenic and lighting design in a theme park.

Scenic designers are nothing new. For over a century they have worked in films, creating the sets that are the backdrop of the production. The history in live theater is far longer. The role they fill in theme parks is much the same. There are important differences though.

Theme park sets are larger than many movie sets. More significantly, they are all-encompassing. In a movie the camera points in only one direction. On a ride our eyes are constantly and motion left, right, up and down.

Like their counterparts in live theater, theme park sets must meet fire and building codes. This applies to both the selection of materials, and the way the materials are used. Often the sets are in an area of the ride that is also as an evacuation area. This must be taken into account by the Set Designer.

Theme park sets must be durable. A Broadway show may last only months, with only a few actors and stage crew ever near the sets. But hundreds of maintenance people over the course of seven or more years will interact with theme park sets.

In a stage show or a film all of the technical junk is offstage. But in a theme park, the sets must conceal speakers, lighting fixtures and sometimes control equipment.

Occasionally stage show sets use forced perspective. The technique is one in which objects that are farther away are rendered much smaller to increase the sensation of vast distances. It is used less often in films. But nearly every theme park ride set incorporates forced perspective to expand the space far beyond the physical boundaries of the scene. It's a complex technique to render believably, and is made more difficult by the fact that the set is viewed from many different angles. Objects that appear far away as you enter a scene must still seem far away as you exit on the opposite side, even though you have moved past them.

Stage shows often use flat sets. But if you're moving past them that doesn't always work in a theme park. And even the best seats in the house are still far away from the sets in a stage show. A little distance can cover a lot of sins. Anyone who is ever seen the sets from a motion picture or television show will know how crude they can be; the camera lens is very forgiving. That's not true in a theme park, where it's not uncommon for the ride vehicle to pass within three or four feet of the sets. That means that rocks need to look like rocks, wood like wood, and metal like metal. Yet no one is going to fill a theme park ride with real rocks, or spend millions of dollars on complicated metalwork. Instead inexpensive wood, fiberglass and other materials are combined, then painted by artists to look—in some cases, anyway—better than the real thing.

Only occasionally do sets in stage shows serve a structural purpose. But in theme parks it's not uncommon for them to provide access to higher levels, so that maintenance personnel can reach lighting fixtures, or reach elevated equipment areas. They're also used to support special effects projectors, fans, and other devices.

Sometimes theme park sets incorporate moving pieces: a giant printing press; window shutters that blow in the wind; or spinning wheels on upended carts.

Theme park sets also use a wider variety of mixed media materials than theater sets. Ultraviolet paint is common—sometimes sets need to completely change appearance when lighting changes from normal to ultraviolet. Theme park sets also incorporate more landscaping: dirt, bushes, trees, even flowing mud.

When they constructed the sets for the queue area of Disneyland's Big Thunder Mountain Railroad, one employee's full-time job was to "age" wood. He spent weeks whacking perfectly good wooden beams with an axe to create the look of wood that had been exposed to the elements for many years. Some cleverly applied paint to add burn marks and water stains, and you've got an instantly decrepit railway.

Most people don't spend a lot of time thinking about lighting. You walk into a room, flip on a switch, and don't give it a second thought. But lighting in a theme park can make a thousand dollar set look like a million bucks.

Halfway through the American Adventure stage show at Epcot, the house is plunged into darkness. We hear the crackle of a fire and the sound of crickets in the wilderness. At center stage a campfire begins to flicker. Standing before it is Chief Joseph, leader of the Nez Perce. He flings his arms wide, and the light of the fire catches the colored stripes of the Indian blanket wrapped about his shoulders. Firelight plays across the crevices of his face as he delivers his famous words, "From where the sun now stands I will fight no more, forever."

What would this scene be without lighting?

Well er, dark. But anyway, you see what I mean. In this case a talented lighting designer took a good scene and made it great.

Far more than in a stage show, lighting in a theme park is up close and personal. It's used to great dramatic effect, to increase the realism of set pieces, and also to reveal different physical elements as the story unfolds, a technique rarely used in live theater or films.

In addition to the creative side of lighting, there is also a technical side, involving control and animation. We will discuss that later, during the engineering portion of this book.

Chapter 16: Media Design

Your vehicle rounds the corner as an explosion rocks it. A brick wall disintegrates. Bricks bombard your vehicle, each impact producing a rapid-fire crack, crack, crack! Twisting around, you surge high above the New York streets, but another impact swings you around, and you are suddenly plummeting faster and faster toward the ground. At the last moment some web-like thing arrests your forward progress and you dangle, nose down, staring at the pavement.

What's going on here?

It's the climax of the Spiderman ride at Universal's Islands of Adventure theme park. From a media production standpoint, this is the world's most complex amusement park ride.

The ultra-realistic experience is created by the perfect synchronization of vehicle motion to 35-mm projectors and onboard surround sound. To get this all to work together is a control system nightmare. But to produce the media was an act of brilliance. Not only does the 3-D film have to match the surrounding sets, it has to match the motion of the vehicle through the sets, since perspective changes from one side of the scene to the other. And the sounds that reinforce the action need to be consistent with the acoustics of the imaginary city streets through which you're flying.

Many, many man-years were spent developing the CGI film and accompanying audio track. And the final product shows it. It's the pinnacle of theme park media design.

The media design process begins with media selection. The most fundamental decision is whether to use film or video. But soon it will seem amazing that we ever used film, just as now it's hard to remember listening to vinyl records (unless you're an audiophile or exceptionally trendy).

Technology has now reached the point where film resolutions can be accomplished using digital projection, which has the advantage of improved mechanical reliability. Many people assume that it's much less expensive to produce a movie digitally rather than on film, but this is not the case. It takes the same field crew to shoot high-definition video as it does film. And the film stock itself is only a minor contributor to end cost. It's true that it costs much less to distribute a film digitally, but that's only an advantage where you're constantly changing the media—something that happens at the neighborhood cinema, but not a theme park.

A major cost factor is the projector bulb, which lasts a surprisingly short period of time in continuous usage. And projector bulbs cost thousands of US dollars each! But both film and digital projection have this drawback.

Theme parks did spend a lot of money replacing film prints—they really only last three to six months. So as digital projection technology improved and projector costs decreased, digital projection became the standard for nearly all theme park presentations.

There's another reason for selecting video over film projection, other than maintenance or cost. Video doesn't need to be presented in linear fashion. This means that interactive shows (or shows were the motion must instantaneously jump to a number of different points depending upon decisions that the audience or control system makes) must be implemented using video media.

A third type of film presentation in theme parks is special effects projection. These are used to create backgrounds of waving wheat, wildfires burning against a sunset sky, rain falling, or clouds floating past. Typically these are either 5x5 or 10x10, where the number reflects the dimensions of the frame in centimeters. In some cases a motor moves the film in front of the lens, creating the effect. In the future most of these effects will be sourced from digital video.

In addition to visual media, Media Designers are also responsible for music and other sounds throughout the attraction. They don't actually compose the music, but they do produce it. For most themed attractions the music must match action, scene length, or vehicle movement. This means—usually—short playback lengths and easily recognized themes.

Most themed attractions also use sound effects and ambience. These are nonmusical sounds that reinforce the experience. Sound effects usually synchronize with observable motions: the clatter of a moving chain, explosions, a hammer pounding a nail. Ambience is background sound that helps set the mood: water lapping against a boat, seagulls crying overhead, the sounds of children in a schoolyard.

The Media Designer's job is to acquire, edit, process, and encode the material, ready for the Audio/Video Engineer's use. Unfortunately this process usually occurs late in the development cycle, and the Audio/Video Engineer often must struggle with last-minute installation of untested media, and hope for the best.

There's one other type of media production that is common: software. Interactives, information terminals, and many exhibits use computer software as audio and visual complements. In this case the responsibility for the development of the end product falls not with the programmers who implement it, but with Media Designers who are skilled in the creation of audio and visual software.

This is a highly specialized field, because it combines both technical and artistic skills. Good media designers are highly paid; they can make millions developing games for home video consoles or cell phones. So it's sometimes difficult to attract top talent for one-of-a-kind theme park projects. Nevertheless some truly stunning results have been produced. Two of my favorites are the Aladdin virtual reality system at DisneyQuest, which was developed by Walt Disney Imagineering, and the Land The Shuttle simulator at Space Center Houston, developed by BRC Imagination Arts and Alcorn McBride.

***

In the past few chapters we looked at the creative disciplines that turn great ideas into great attractions. Art Directors, Show Producers, Set and Lighting Designers, plus Film, Video and Audio Media Designers all work together to produce a truly great attraction. They are the primary force that moves the project from Blue Sky to the first phases of technical design. Although their involvement continues until the grand opening, they have the most freedom while the project is still in the creative stages. As technical design begins, it becomes a lot harder—and more expensive—to change things.

This is the point at which the Theme Park Engineers enter the arena, tiny Davids ready to take on a Goliath named "The Project". Next, we'll take a detailed look at each stage of the project, and you will see that the creative design is just one aspect of the giant task that looms over us. We'll do our best not to get stepped on.

Bear in mind that this step is your last chance for creative input, unfettered by work that the technical people have—sometimes literally—cast in concrete. From here on, creative changes become much more expensive.

So watch your step as you enter the moving vehicle. The lap bar will lower automatically.

Chapter 17: Getting Started

At the end of Epcot's China film, the wizened old philosopher advises us, "Even a journey of a thousand miles begins with a single step." He was speaking of a trip along the Great Wall of China, a distance only slightly longer than the walk to your car in the Epcot parking lot.

Just like walking the Great Wall, theme park projects of immense size begin with a few simple actions. But the journey is long, and the traveler will encounter many strangers along the way.

In the next few chapters we're going to sprint through nearly all of the phases of a major theme park project, from initial concept through the early stages of design and construction, then installation and test, and finally a—hopefully—grand opening to the public. Along the way we'll encounter strangers beyond the creative and engineering disciplines to whom you've already been introduced. Many of these folks have professions that will only be mentioned in passing during the remainder of this book. But now is our chance to see them in action.

At the end of this sprint you will have an appreciation for the many diverse people who work on theme parks. Perhaps you'll see yourself in one of these roles. If so, that's a great clue to what your own involvement in theme parks might be as a career.

This is our last chance to take a look at the big picture and to "play" outside of the area of our expertise—Theme Park Design. From here on we're going to pay more attention to the workings of the attraction. But for now let's see what it takes to get to opening day.

We already looked at the conceptual process from the Creative Team's standpoint. There is more to the initial conception of a theme park attraction than just what the Creative Team does. There's even a stage before the Creative Team begins.

In The Beginning

It may seem obvious, but the first step in the creation of the new theme park attraction is for someone in management to decide they need a new attraction. That seems basic, but there are many considerations involved. What is the park's current attendance? What will its attendance be if no new attractions are added? How well are the old attractions holding up, both from an artistic and maintenance standpoint? Is there sufficient money or financing available to build a new attraction? What sort of attraction would bring the kind of people the park is looking for?

To some extent the public actually determines this process by their preferences. But it is management's reaction to public preference that initiates the whole process. It would be rare management that went to the Creative Team and said, "We need a new attraction. Come up with something."

A more likely approach is for management to tell the Creative Team, "We need an attraction that appeals to the six to ten-year-old age group," or, "It's too hot at our theme park during the summer. We need an attraction that cools people off by getting them wet."

The Creative Team can now nurture this seed of an idea until it grows up to be a Sequoia. Or a zucchini.

Blue Sky

Before we only talked about the Creative Team's Blue Sky process. We ignored the aspects of Blue Sky that other disciplines undertake. There's an interaction with management at this point because the Creative Team won't fully develop any idea until management has approved it. Instead, the Creative Team throws 10 or 15 quick ideas at management to see which ones "stick to wall". Sometimes sticking to the wall is literal. Ideas are posted on bulletin boards and those passing by give their gut reaction.

Blue Sky can also involve the technical disciplines. It would be a foolish management team that embarked on their favorite creative idea without checking with the engineers to get a general idea of how much it will cost. It's all well and good to suggest taking guests to the moon as a big draw for your space theme park. But if the art directors intend to REALLY take people to the moon it could get rather expensive.

Obviously, that's an exaggeration. But it's easy for engineers to estimate budget for a project based upon its creative content.

One reason it's easy is that no one expects them to be right at this point. If they're smart, they'll inflate the cost by a factor of three, because we all know that the Creative Team will get lots of expensive ideas for improvements as we go along. Still, inflated or not, these numbers are useful for comparing the relative costs of different proposals.

Estimating (and repeat)

This is where the trouble starts. What if management just LOVES that go to the moon idea, but doesn't love the engineer's estimate that goes along with it?

Re-estimate it, obviously.

This is where the professional bean counters come in and try to figure out how to get the engineers to make it cheaper. Typically, they take a whole bunch of appealing stuff out of the original idea, and try to do what's left in the least expensive—and lowest quality—manner. The unfortunate results of this process are:

Management becomes convinced that the project can be done economically.

The Creative Team realizes that they're going to end up with an awful attraction unless they can find a way to slip back in all the expensive stuff that was taken out to save money.

The Maintenance guys realize that they're going to end up with an attraction built on such a shoestring budget and they won't be able to keep it running.

Later on, the final results are:

Management is furious when they discover that the attraction ends up costing just what the engineers predicted in the first place; that figure was three times what they wanted to spend.

The Creative Team is unhappy with all the fixes they had to put in to try to compensate for the good stuff that was taken out at the beginning.

But the Maintenance team is happy. They've all quit and gone to work for a different park, anyway.

But I'm getting ahead of myself.

Chapter 18: Design

At some point someone makes the decision to build something. A project may have languished in creative development for years, waiting for a champion in management to back it. Or it may have been fast-tracked to tie in with an upcoming and—hopefully—blockbuster movie release. In either event, we've now got the bulk of the creative design done, funded the "hard" design, and turned on the guys who really know how to spend money.

Facilities Design

The largest single consumer of budget in a themed attraction (unless it's a rehab of an existing attraction, or an outdoor ride) is almost invariably the building itself. Site work, infrastructure (utilities and such), steel and concrete cost a heap of money—as much as $50 million or more for a complex attraction. Then there are interior walls, finishing, flooring, paint, electrical, plumbing, lighting, emergency lighting, and so on.

The point is, all of this stuff has to be designed sometime by somebody. Well now is the time; and the architects, architectural engineers and facilities engineers are the somebodies. It's not uncommon for the architectural design alone to cost several million dollars. And that's just the paperwork.

Think about it: a 160-foot self-supporting geodesic sphere anchored by three pillars, with a few million pounds of ride in it. Got one of those in your neighborhood?

Didn't think so. But somebody had to make Spaceship Earth stand up, even during hurricanes. That costs money.

You might assume that the show and ride had to be defined before a building could be designed to house them. That's not really the case. The process is somewhat parallel, and major requirements of the interior design do impact the exterior structure. But more often the building constrains the show or ride. That's because construction rushes ahead to stay on the immutable, omnipotent schedule, even while the attraction is being designed and redesigned.

To give you an idea of just how much can change during a project, look at American Adventure. This Epcot pavilion features a theatrical show with a bunch of fourteen-foot-high lifts that carry animated figures from a pit up to stage level. Because different figures must appear in the same spot at various times, the lifts must be rearranged during the show. This is accomplished using a 400,000-pound carriage containing the lifts. Noiselessly, it rolls beneath the audience, indexing to the correct spot for each scene. Obviously this had a major impact on the building. And yet, when construction of the building began it was believed that the lifts would be mounted on a giant turntable!

Art Direction

We've seen that Art Direction begins during Blue Sky. It doesn't end until the last roll of wallpaper is glued on. Depending upon the budget—and the Art Director—the results (and the cost) can vary widely. But a great Art Director can be the difference between a lackluster attraction and a truly great one.

Want that special paint that doesn't fade in the sun? Synthetic fabric not realistic enough for your animatronics wardrobe? Oh, now that we're using real silk, we have to fireproof it. And of course fake rocks cost more than the real thing.

A big part of the budget goes to those little details that can be so important.

Or not. When Thomas Jefferson and Ben Franklin rise on stage in American Adventure, I doubt that anybody notices that all those crumpled up drafts of the Declaration of Independence are just that.

But it makes a good story.

Technical Design

This is what this book is about. Other than a few estimates—and some advise that was probably ignored—this is our first chance as Theme Park Engineers to sink our teeth into that zucchini—er, project. However, like any great chef, I'm going to make you smell the wonderful aromas emanating from the kitchen just a little bit longer before I serve the main course. For now we're going to skip right over the technical design and start building stuff.

Chapter 19: Construction

How hard could it be to build a building? Just because it's a shape no one's ever seen before, doesn't make it difficult. And those materials no one's ever used before, they should be no problem. And the plans that keep changing every—what's that? Another new set? Let me have a look at those. Yeah, yeah, we can do it. It'll just take an extra month or so.

What do you mean 'You're pulling the schedule in?" Are you listening!?

Sigh.

Excuse me, I have to get back to the site.

Chapter 20: Commissioning

It was the night the curtains went berserk that I decided we wouldn't make opening day. I had been sitting in the American Adventure pit watching one of the engineers program the stage control system. Suddenly there were cries from above me on the proscenium and other voices shouting out from the darkness around me. I looked up and saw that the main curtain—an incredibly complicated affair with individual wires that could lift different sections to different positions, and that probably cost half a million dollars—was raising and lowering in scatterbrained craziness. Off to the side, smaller fly curtains were also going up and down wildly. And several heavy overhead scrims were attempting to drop. Derek, one of the Show Control Engineers, ran for the curtain control room and madly hit every stop button he could find.

Later, examining the animation cabinets, we saw that we were being flooded with bad data from Epcot Central. The problem was traced to a faulty transmitter at the other end of a half-mile of cabling. The card was swapped out.

It took days to unsnarl the main curtain.

Programming and Animation

While the engineers down in the pit sweat out the details of programming the computers that run the ride and show, a completely different kind of programming was going on upstairs in the theater. Up there, skilled—and specialized—artists worked at an animation console, adjusting the way the Animatronic figures move. They'd run the show—or small sections of the show—over and over, tweaking and adjusting controls one by one to match the soundtrack and to make the movements as realistic as possible.

It's an arduous process, because for each figure they must learn its mechanical limitations and then take advantage of them. Sometimes a hip twist can provide the extra momentum needed to make that arm movement look just right. But then the figure is turned the wrong way for the next move. It took weeks to get Ben Franklin to convincingly climb a short flight of stairs.

All that while we sat downstairs, chafing at not being able to move the sets and get our own work done.

But there's always the night

Test and Adjust

WANTED: Engineers to work 18 hour shifts seven days a week for three months. Sleeping accommodations (dark, oil-soaked pit) provided. All the theme park hamburgers you can eat. Please be sure to fill out your time sheet for 40 hours; we don't pay overtime.

Test and adjust. Those two little words make it sound so easy. See if it works, if not turn the knob. But there are tens of thousands of interrelated knobs any one of which has the potential to bring your attraction to its knees. And of course all that knob fiddling is done by exhausted individuals in an impossibly compressed time span.

So if it takes so long, why not schedule an appropriate amount of time to test and adjust from the start?

We did. The problem is that there are two certainties in any theme park project schedule:

One is that the schedule will slip.

The other is that opening day won't change.

Since test and adjust is the last activity before opening day... well, you get the idea. I've worked on projects where the scheduled time for test and adjust became negative! See if Einstein can figure that one out.

Test and adjust at its best is an exhilarating time. It's a time to get speeds just right. A time to test the reliability of sensors and maybe move them an inch or two. A time to make sure that water doesn't overflow boat troughs and turn down the pumps if it does. A time to laugh when you discover the electrical conduits have been filled with water by those overflowing troughs

But what if the whole approach doesn't work? What if that system of a dozen high-pressure valves can't raise that lift in ten seconds no matter how you actuate them?

Then test and adjust turns into "insanely chaotic field redesign and punt'.

Anyway, that's how we spent the last few months in American Adventure: changing valves, changing wiring, reprogramming stage computers, and always trying to keep things from running into each other or tearing each other apart.

One day we actuated the valves on Thomas Jefferson's and Ben Franklin's lift in the wrong order and managed to put 30 degree bend into a steel I-beam the size of your leg. Ten minutes later the welders were cutting the piece out and replacing it. Time waits for no theme park opening.

Opening

The first American Adventure show was presented to the public on an employee preview night, four days before opening. Most of the Epcot team had heard rumors that it might run—go 102 in Disney parlance. When we finally put out the radio call "American Adventure 102" hundreds of people had already gathered in the preshow area outside the theater doors. Many of the executives were there.

Of course, just as there's a 102, there is also the dreaded 101: the attraction going down in ignominious flames, so to speak. My fingers were crossed.

At least half the audience knew how complex a show it was—by far the most complex Disney had ever attempted. They also knew that it had never run successfully. A lift had always failed to appear, or the carriage stopped short of its marks. Down in the pit I could almost feel their good will, as if the lifts were being willed up by psychic energy.

One by one the lifts rose, and the carriage indexed. Near the end, when Walt Disney's face appeared on the screen, the theater filled with spontaneous applause. When the show was over there was a standing ovation.

Tweaking

That was the last successful show for days. We discovered that if we let the hydraulic oil cool off, the timing was thrown off just enough to bring things to a stop. Other stuff broke. And things that had once worked suddenly refused to cooperate. A cable was sabotaged by a disgruntled construction worker. And sleep-deprived engineers even managed to start a small fire by shorting out a 110 volt line.

To keep the oil warm I dozed fitfully through the night before Epcot's grand opening, constantly restarting the show. By morning, when Electronic Project Engineer Glenn Birket came in to relieve me, I was so tired I went home and slept through opening day. Later I learned that my sleepless night was for naught. By mid-morning the attraction was down, and would not rise again that day.

"American Adventure 101" the radio call went out, again and again that first month, but with—fortunately—decreasing frequency. Also fortunately, we were not alone. The Energy Pavilion and Spaceship Earth, both also mechanically complex, were having their own problems. But there was plenty of other stuff to see in the park. Fortunately my wife's projects—a ride and a half dozen theaters— were all working flawlessly.

More hundred hour weeks, but with a bit more sleep here and there, some mechanical fixes that worked, and a gradually developed understanding of the REAL—as opposed to theoretical—design criteria led to improved systems, software and reliability. By the second month we were operating at 98% readiness.

Of course, the downside of the attraction working is that it's open to the public all day. This means finishing your tweaking in the middle of the night. On the other hand, I suppose I'd rather work all night than all day AND all night.

By year-end we were at nearly 100% readiness.

Renovation

Perhaps that sounds like the end of the story.

It's not.

In the words of Walt Disney, "As long as there is imagination in the hearts of men, Disneyland will never be finished."

Neither will Epcot.

Twelve years after American Adventure's shaky opening, the attraction was rehabbed. New animatronic figures, new figure controllers, new lift valves, and a new lift control system replaced all that equipment we'd sweated blood for.

The new show is bigger, better, and more reliable than the old. The experience gained in ten years of maintenance and monitoring audience response was well used.

Am I sad that my work ended up in the Property Control boneyard? Yes and no. I entertained millions of people during those ten years. American Adventure provided a moving—and cool—place to spend a half hour during a visit to Epcot. That show was the diamond of the park, once it worked. It still is.

And I can't really hold a grudge against the Show Control Engineer who obsoleted it.

She's my wife.

✳✳✳

In the past few chapters we've looked at all the stages of project development, from Blue Sky through Grand Opening. I focused on the last stages—the final years anyway—of design, construction and commissioning. I've chosen to emphasize this period because it's where we spend most of our effort, it's the most interesting, and it's the most rewarding.

I've put you all vicariously on the Epcot site during the last few months prior to opening and let you experience the chaos, the despair, and the triumph of building a great theme park. That's what this business is all about.

Next we'll focus our attention on the engineers. We'll survey the different engineering disciplines involved in theme park engineering, in preparation for the remainder of the book, where we focus on one type of engineer in each section.

Until then, please check the area around you to make sure that you have all of your personal possessions before leaving the vehicle.

Chapter 21: Meet The Engineers

My father was an engineer.

My mother worked for an engineering company.

Through round after round of aerospace layoffs during the 1960s my mother constantly warned me, "Don't be an engineer. Engineers have no job security. Engineers have to work crazy hours. You'll never make any money. Engineers never do anything interesting."

So, of course, I became an engineer.

But I guess I spent so much time trying not to be an engineer, I ended up with a fairly broad range of interests. Or maybe I'm just nosy. In any event, I've always kept my eyes open and been interested in what everyone around me was doing. Perhaps that's important if you want to be a good engineer.

Fortunately, my mother was wrong about a few things. With society's changing emphasis on technology, engineers now have pretty good job security—almost the opposite of the situation in the 1960s. Engineers also make pretty good money these days, particularly if they work in a specialized field. And I think even aerospace engineering is interesting, although theme park engineering beats it by a mile.

She was right about one thing though: we do work crazy hours.

We've taken a pretty thorough look at the process of creating a theme park attraction in the preceding chapters. Now that you have a good understanding of the overall task, we're going to focus our attention on the engineering disciplines that make that attraction work.

First we'll survey the different engineering disciplines and describe, in general terms, what they do. Then we'll take a detailed look at each of those engineering specialties, and see how they impact your attraction.

Speaking of your attraction, it had better be pretty well defined at this point. As engineers we're going to start spending money on some rather large, expensive things—buildings for example—and it's going to get progressively expensive to make creative changes. So take off your funny looking creative hat (the one with the moose antlers), and put on your hardhat. We're headed for the construction site.

Types of Engineers

There are nearly as many different types of engineers as there are types of science: chemical engineers, nuclear engineers, petroleum engineers, the list goes on. We're not going to talk about any of those. We're going to restrict ourselves to those engineering disciplines commonly used to design and build theme parks.

Theme Park Engineers can be divided into three general groups: mechanical, electrical, and managerial. An analogy is the simplest way to illustrate the differences.

Perhaps you know someone in your neighborhood who is interested in model railroading. Maybe they have friends who get together on weekends to set up sawhorses in the garage. On top of the sawhorses they place a four foot by eight foot sheet of plywood on which one of them is constructing hills and mountains, villages and forests, and is in the process of installing 100 feet of tiny rails, lovingly attaching each section to its roadbed using authentic spikes. That guy's a Mechanical, Structural or Architectural Engineer.

The other guy spends his day lying on his back underneath the board fiddling with wires that energize individual sections of track. These wires all go to a black box filled with circuit boards and more wires. No one is quite sure what the black box does, but every once in a while sparks come out of one side, or smoke comes out of the top. That guy's an Electrical, Electronic, or Software Engineer.

There's a third person in this analogy. She's the woman who comes down the steps from the house into the garage and says, "Get that board out of the way! It's about to rain and I need to put my car back in the garage." She's the Project Manager.

In the next few chapters we're going to meet all of these people.

You go ahead. I'll catch up as soon as I've put this board away.

Chapter 22: Building Castles

The little boy who spent the day building sand castles at the beach, or the little girl who always disassembled her Barbie doll to see how the joints work: they're the kind of people who grow up to be mechanical, structural or architectural engineers.

Mechanical Engineers

Anyone who likes to spend an evening disassembling his automobile's engine is going to love spending the day designing a ride vehicle.

Mechanical engineers who work in theme parks work with slightly different constraints than most mechanical engineers. In the real world, mechanical products are generally classified as high-volume or low-volume.

An example of a high volume product is the transmission of your car; there are millions. High-volume products tend to be carefully designed, sparing no expense, to guarantee that each will cost as little as possible to produce. Given the competitive nature of the automobile industry, every dollar counts, particularly when you multiply it by millions of units.

A low volume product is something like the crawler that moves the space shuttle from the vehicle assembly building to the launch pad; there are only a few. Low-volume and one-of-a-kind items are generally built without many cost constraints, but may not be intended for repetitive wear and tear applications. That crawler may only make a few hundred trips during a twenty-year lifespan.

Theme park attractions are different. They require mechanical designs that are produced in relatively low volume at moderate cost that will be extraordinarily durable and reliable. Unlike high-volume products, anything needed for a theme park must be developed quickly, without years of research and testing before deployment. And unlike the shuttle crawler, theme park mechanical designs are used several times a minute.

Here's an example. The brake mechanism on a roller coaster must be extremely reliable. Yet that vehicle goes around the track in under three minutes, loads in two minutes, then does it again, all day long. But the guy who designed it had a staff of three and less than 18 months from conception to deployment. That requires some careful and competent engineering.

The tight time frames and small staffs involved in theme park design might lead you to suspect that theme park designs are not all that complicated. That is far from the case.

Here's another example. Rides like Disney's Haunted Mansion use a propulsion mechanism called an Omnimover. It consists of a continuous, motor-driven chain that drags the vehicles around a ride track with almost any horizontal or vertical profile. Cams on the underside of the vehicles cause them to rotate into desired orientations at various spots around the ride. There may also be cams or fingers that trigger audio or cause mechanical actions such as lowering the lap bars.

Rides like this contain thousands of moving parts. Yet the system was designed by a small staff of mechanical engineers in a short period of time. It has proven highly reliable in over 40 years of nearly continuous use.

While the majority of mechanical engineering in theme parks involves wheels and vehicles, Theme Park Mechanical Engineers also work with water pumps, electrical winches, and hydraulic lifts, plus anything else it might take to satisfy those crazy Art Directors.

Architectural Engineers

Just as Art Directors come up with ideas that challenge the Mechanical Engineers, they also challenge Architectural Engineers. Theme park buildings may have huge cantilevered spaces, or be made from unusual materials, or not even look like buildings.

But then again, so may the neighborhood shopping mall. So you might think architectural engineering for theme parks is a lot like architectural engineering elsewhere. But shopping malls are rarely built on reclaimed land, rarely have to withstand the constant vibration induced by careening ride vehicles, and almost never need a roof structure strong enough to support catwalks laden with lighting and special effects equipment.

It's important to understand the basic difference between an architectural engineer and an architect. Many architects are engineers. But not all. The differences this: an architect is responsible for designing a building that suits the owner's needs; an architectural engineer is responsible for making sure that it stays standing.

As with Theme Park Mechanical Engineers, Theme Park Architectural Engineers must work on tight time frames, yet create innovative spaces that meet both the Art Director's expectations and the local building codes. They must work carefully and competently to achieve exciting and yet safe results.

Structural and Civil Engineers

What about all that big stuff that isn't a building? Roads, bridges, lagoons, even parking lots are the domain of Structural and Civil Engineers. That stuff may not seem as exciting as some of the other elements of theme park design, but it's just as important.

When Walt Disney World was developed, the first step in taming 44,000 acres of swamp was creating a canal system that would allow the land to drain. And the second step was creating roads so the construction site could be accessed. That work continues to this day.

Civil Engineers at theme parks perform a parallel role to that in any big city. They do site planning, transportation studies, and energy distribution. They're also responsible for environmental issues including wetlands preservation, water use, and waste disposal.

Sometimes the requirements are just like those of a small city. Other times they can be far different. Relatively few employees commute to a theme park. But 40,000 or 50,000 visitors may arrive by car in just a couple of hours. And unlike commuters, none of them knows where they're going! So theme park traffic signs need to be a lot better than those on the interstate highway.

When Disney decided to build Walt Disney World, one of the first things they did was to get the Florida legislature to make their vast property into its own pseudo-county, the Reedy Creek Development District. This gave them a rare opportunity to try new ways of doing things with a fresh building code. For example, underneath the Magic Kingdom they created a network of "Utilidors" for the distribution of food, services, and as a way for employees to easily move about "backstage".

Along the ceiling of these corridors runs plumbing, electrical circuits, control wiring and the innovative "AVACS" system. Basically, it's a giant vacuum cleaner. At various spots around the Magic Kingdom there are trashcan-like receptacles that employees use for waste disposal. But they're connected to a quarter mile of tubes that lead to the energy plant behind the Magic Kingdom. Close the lid on the receptacle and your trash is sucked out of the Happiest Place on Earth and into the trashiest place on earth.

AVACS was a pretty ambitious and revolutionary bit of civil engineering. To really work, the system had to be powerful—so powerful that they tested it using automotive batteries. And a system that powerful has to be safe. Interlocks prevent the vacuum from engaging if any lid is open. The necessity for this was demonstrated clearly one day. A hatch was left open on receptacle inside a small shed. When the vacuum came on the entire shed turned into a wad of crumpled aluminum! (My vote for worst job in the world: the little guy who has to slide on a cart through the tubes, cleaning out blockages.)

The other revolutionary aspect of AVACS was what was at the other end: an energy plant where trash was turned into energy to help power the park. You'll note my use of the past tense. Unfortunately, like many innovative systems, the energy plant cost more than it saved, and it was abandoned in the 1980s for much cheaper electricity purchased from outside sources. But you've got to admire them for trying.

Chapter 23: Don't Trip Over That Cord

If it moves, it probably needs to be controlled. That's what Ride Control and Show Control Engineers spend a lot of their time doing. They (and a number of other folks who spend their lives trying to avoid electrocution) are the subject of this chapter.

Ride Control Engineers

Sitting in a half-darkened alcove, the Ride Control Engineer surveys the vehicle load area before him. The Mechanical Engineers have cleared the track. The vehicle sits in the Dispatch Area, gleaming under the bright worklights. The air smells of lubricant and hot rubber tires.

The Ride Control engineer—who looks and dresses almost exactly like James Bond, by the way—checks the lines on his computer screen one last time, takes a final drag on the expensive imported cigarette dangling from his lower lip, and then lifts a walkie-talkie to his mouth. (Unfortunately this knocks the cigarette out of his mouth onto the computer keyboard, where it starts a small fire, but it is quickly extinguished. Ride Control Engineers live for danger.)

"Ready for launch," he says in a voice tight with nervous tension.

"Clear," comes the tinny reply from others out on the ride track.

The Ride Control Engineer taps a key.

With a squeal, the vehicle erupts from the dispatch area and leaps toward the first scene. Fourteen feet later is crosses a zone boundary, the brakes lock all four wheels, and it slides to a stop in a cloud of burning rubber.

The Ride Control Engineer—who actually looks more like Harry Potter, now that I think about it—sighs, slumps in his chair, and squints at the computer screen with a look that clearly says the machine is guilty of the most shameful betrayal.

It's going to be a long night.

It takes nerves of steel to be a ride control engineer. Also a sharp intellect, and good analytical skills, because the safety of—literally—millions of people is dependent upon the Ride Control Engineer.

This safety is achieved in a number of ways. The most common technique is redundancy: more than one computer making decisions about the ride. If the computers disagree, the ride E-Stops—industry parlance for an emergency stop, a controlled event that brings things to a motionless safe state as quickly as possible.

Most Ride Control Engineers are expert at Failure Modes and Effects analysis. Using this technique, every single monitoring or control point in a ride is analyzed to see what the result would be if it failed. Single and multiple point failure analysis and formal Safety Acceptance Testing are also essential.

Finally, if the ride is to be a good one, the Ride Control Engineer must assure that it has the motion profile the Art Directors intended, and that it is properly synchronized to other systems.

As you can see, Ride Control Engineering is one of the most demanding yet rewarding careers in Theme Park Design. Particularly if you have the soul of James Bond but are trapped Harry Potter's body.

Show Control Engineers

With more variety and less stress than ride control, Show Control Engineering gets my vote as most interesting job. Where else can you find a job where you get to control dancing alligators, bubbling lava, and singing broccoli—possibly all in the same day?

The show control engineer has a hand in nearly everything that you experience from the moment you enter an attraction.

Let's put on our Show Control Engineering hard hat and walk through a simple theater attraction. Here's how the Show Control Engineer views it:

As we enter the preshow doors, we pass through an electronic turnstile were an infrared beam counts us and displays the number of people in the preshow area on a small display near the Operator Control Console (OCC). Over there on the wall, designed to fit into the themed paneling, the countdown clocks tells us there are 18 minutes until the next main show. The background music in here has been running continuously since it was started by the show control system early in the morning, providing a general ambiance. That was also when the show control system set the lighting levels.

Ten minutes before the main show begins, the show control system fades out the background music and starts a video that runs on monitors in the preshow area. The show control engineer makes a note to bring the lighting levels down a bit more to make the video easier to see. Periodically the hostess needs to ask people to move all the way to the front to make room for more. When she does, she presses a button on the microphone. This causes the show control system to automatically "duck" the soundtrack and mix in the microphone audio.

As main showtime nears, the show control system fades up a spotlight to illuminate the preshow hostess and patches the microphone audio through to the overhead speakers. The hostess introduces the show. Partway through her spiel a cue light on the OCC warns her that the main show is about to end. She cautions the guests to remain behind the yellow line until the doors open. A moment later the show control system flashes the "Caution: Automatic Doors" sign above the entryway. After a few seconds' delay it commands the door controller to open the doors.

The audience begins to file through the entry doors even as the previous audience is leaving through the exit doors on the other side of the theater. The show control system has set the theater houselights to bright so people can see clearly. It has also started the fill/spill music in the theater which is a perfectly synced continuation of the music in the preshow. The show control engineer is pleased.

After a minute or two the show control system commands the theater exit doors to close, and in another minute the theater entrance doors also close. OCCs near both sets of doors allow the operators to override these automatic actions if needed.

Once everyone is seated, the hostess at the front of the theater presses a button on an OCC to tell the show control system to start the main show. As she gives her introductory spiel, the show control system starts up the projectors and audio source and ensures that they remain locked together in perfect synchronization throughout the entire 20 minute show.

The houselights gradually fade to darkness. The audience waits in breathless anticipation—the show control engineer strains to hear confirmation that the projector's film transport is ramping up in the back of the theater. As the hostess completes her spiel the curtains are commanded to open. Once the screen is exposed, the show control system opens the projector dousers (shutters that allow light to fall onto the screen) at the exact moment that the movie begins. For the audience the main entertainment is just beginning. But for the show control engineer the action is pretty much over.

Sometime during the movie, out in the preshow the cycle begins again.

At the completion of the movie the process is reversed: the house lights come up, the curtains close, the exit doors open, and the guests Exit Through Retail.

And that was a simple show! Imagine all the buttons, lights, wires and logic it took to do that, plus handle unusual conditions such as building-wide pages, fire alarms, failed projectors, and curtains that overshot their mark.

More than any other single individual, the show control engineer understands how the entire attraction operates. But never, ever take one of these people with you to see a Broadway show.

Audio/Video Engineers

With the show control engineer responsible for controlling all that audio and video, you might be wondering what the Audio/Video Engineers do.

They source it, process it, amplify it, and deliver it.

Theme park audio generally doesn't come from tape recorders or CD players. The devices used to playback audio in a theme Park must work for years without any maintenance—not even dusting. So mostly they are solid-state. The best units use the same kind of storage card that you might plug into your digital camera.

Similarly, video must also require no maintenance for years. Most theme park video players use magnetic disks to store high performance digital video.

As we've seen from our description of show control engineers, there are many different audio zones with different control requirements: looping, synchronization to movies, microphones, etc. The Audio/Video Engineer connects all of these sources to some sort of digital processing equipment that can be used to alter levels and frequency response, and mix and route the audio to different areas.

The output of this audio processor is then connected to the amplifiers. From there it is distributed around the building. The types of amplifiers and distribution vary depending upon use.

Video is sourced and distributed similarly. Video monitors, flat panel displays and digital projectors must be selected for appropriate size and brightness.

The audio video engineer also specifies all of the speakers. There are many different types of speakers in a single attraction. Overhead ceiling speakers are common in the preshow. A full range of speakers —from subwoofers to horns—are used in the main show. And outdoors there may even be speakers disguised as rocks!

To select the amplifiers and speakers the Audio/Video Engineer needs to understand something about the acoustics of the spaces in the building. This is not to say that Audio/Video Engineers are acousticians. This function is usually performed by a specialist, or by the architectural engineering firm. They are the ones who select the acoustical treatments in the building. (Project management then deletes most of them because they are deemed frivolous and expensive and "you can't see them anyhow".) The Audio/Video Engineer must deal with the result.

Audio/Video Engineering is a great career choice for someone who spends his or her weekends drooling over expensive hi-fi equipment at the local stereo store. In the early days of theme parks, audio systems and acoustics were afterthoughts. But in the past 20 years a demanding public expects superior audio performance. That means lots of expensive toys for the Audio/Video Engineer in spite of the project manager.

Lighting Designers

Nearly every stage show has a lighting designer, and it might seem that lighting design for theme parks would be little different than ordinary stage lighting. This may be true in the case of live shows, but most theme park attractions are static and highly automated. This means that exactly the correct lighting fixture can be selected for each feature that is to be illuminated. And theme park Lighting Designers aren't just "throwing" light. Often the fixtures themselves become a part of the theming.

Theme park attractions use a wide variety of esoteric lighting fixtures: spotlights, architectural lighting, spark tubes, liquid neon, strobes, lasers, and fiber optics are all common.

In the live theater a lighting fixture may only be on for a few minutes a day. In a theme park it will be on for years. This means that careful selection of lamp type and color filter are essential in order to keep down maintenance costs, and keep the same "look" year after year.

Special Effects Designers

The Special Effects Designers probably isn't an engineer. He's more likely a guy who grew up reading surplus catalogs, disassembling firecrackers, and dyeing his sister's pigtails green using his junior chemistry kit. Nevertheless, if his pants are too short, he wears a pocket protector, or eats sufficient quantities of Twinkies we'll award him an honorary engineering credential and include him here.

A lot of what Special Effects Designers do is engineering. A lot more is trial and error. Their methods are not so rigorous, nor their results as predictable as we engineers might like. But their designs may incorporate electronics, chemistry, lighting or mechanical systems, so a certain amount of technical knowledge is a must.

Special effects are normally prototyped long before the attraction is built, because they must measure up to the dreams of the Art Director. Among the minor miracles they're asked to perform: lava that bubbles endlessly, cigars that smoke day after day, and buildings that burn forever.

Gee, that's all pretty hot stuff.

But they also might need to come up with: blocks of ice that don't melt, rain that falls ceaselessly, or a ceiling that simulates the roiling surface of the ocean.

They've also been called upon to simulate the smells of roses, hot rocks, and stinkbugs. One particularly nasty smelling bottle in the special effects lab was labeled "Troll Crotch".

I leave it to your imagination.

Chapter 24: Who's The Boss?

There's an old saying that too many cooks spoil the broth. If a theme park attraction were a kitchen it would be pretty crowded, and not just with cooks. A lot of those people milling around would be trying to manage the cooks. In fact, now that I look more closely, I only see one cook. And about ten managers.

Well, with all that supervision, this broth should really be delicious.

Of course, if this really were a themed attraction, the Art Director would show up five minutes before dinner and decide he wanted chili instead.

Anyway, here are a few of the people trying to plan our menu:

Systems Engineers

While the Show Control Engineer may understand how most of the attraction works in microscopic detail, the Systems Engineer is the guy responsible for making sure it works at some higher level.

If you like sitting at a lab bench doing experiments, or designing things on paper and then seeing them "in the flesh", then you'd hate being a Systems Engineer. On the other hand, if you like to look at the big picture and hate getting caught up in annoying little details, then Systems Engineering is a perfect career choice.

A lot of what Systems Engineers do is similar to what Coordinators do: they make sure people communicate. But unlike Coordinators, Systems Engineers operate on a technical level. They understand what the Mechanical, Electrical, and Electronic Engineers are trying to accomplish and they make sure those disciplines understand each other's needs.

This can save a lot of money if—when everyone gets to the field —things work together as intended.

I've often seen attractions where the behavior of the mechanical parts—which seemed so obvious to the Mechanical Engineer—is completely different than what the control systems engineers expected. As a result, weeks of time are wasted trying to re-architect the software or add new electronics to deal with a behavior that the Mechanical Engineer knew about all along.

A good System Engineer prevents this from happening.

The Systems Engineer evaluates trade-offs, determining whether more money should be spent on the mechanical system to make the control systems simpler and cheaper, or if more money should be spent on the control system allowing for a less expensive mechanical design.

Systems Engineering is a relatively new approach to theme park attractions design. Sometimes it works, sometimes not. I've seen Systems Engineers accomplish next to nothing over the course of a three-year project. But I've also seen them save the project millions of dollars by anticipating problems before they occurred and solving them while it was still inexpensive.

Project Engineers

Project engineers are theoretically in charge of all engineering on a theme park project. This means everything from buildings standing up to the ride working to exit signs lighting and even toilets flushing. It's all under their jurisdiction.

This may sound like a terrific responsibility, and it is.

In practice, Project Engineers tend to focus on where the money gets spent. That means the building. As a result most Project Engineers are "steel and concrete guys". This means that they know little about control systems, they rarely become involved in audio or video, and don't regard special effects as an engineering discipline at all.

Because they spend most of their time working with the architects and construction companies, those of us who are focused on making the attraction work seldom have much to do with the Project Engineer. But it's an important role, and one which has the potential of saving the company more money than the entire cost of the control system or audio installation.

It's easy to get Project Engineering confused with Project Management, and even its relationship to Systems Engineering can be fuzzy. In a nutshell, the differences are this:

The Systems Engineer is responsible for making sure that the mechanical electrical and electronic systems function together. His concern is with the ride and show content of the attraction. It does not involve structural engineering.

The Project Engineer is responsible for all engineering activities, but focuses on structural issues.

The Project Manager is responsible for the overall project, but he or she does not have an engineering degree. It's the Project Manager who makes sure the checks get signed.

So who is the boss?

A lot of people working together make a theme park attraction happen.

As engineers our ultimate boss is the Project Engineer, who paradoxically has little interest in most of what we call Theme Park Design.

Collectively, the big boss is the Project Manager. He or she is responsible for all aspects of the attraction, and reports directly to Corporate Management.

But in the end the boss is... You.

As a Theme Park Engineer, you are ultimately responsible for your own systems. In the mad rush that always occurs to complete an attraction, no one can second-guess you.

You have to make the right decisions or the attraction won't open on time.

Down to Specifics

So far we've taken a broad tour of all the different Theme Park Design disciplines, from the guys who make the building stand up, to the people who fill it with the smell of stinkbugs.

It's a wide field, and there's something here to interest nearly everyone.

In the chapters that follow we'll take a more detailed look at some of the most interesting Theme Park Design disciplines, and find out how they can help us design our attraction.

But for now, please go all the way to the end of the aisle, filling every available seat to make room for others.

Chapter 25: The Show Control Engineer

We've arrived at the meat of the book. The appetizers and salad were fun, but now we've got some real work to do. Now we'll put on our Show Control Engineer's (hard) hat and get down to the real work of designing a theme park attraction.

You graduated from college with a degree in Electronic Engineering. Now, with the ink on your diploma barely dry, you're sitting in your cubicle at a Fortune 500 company. Or maybe it's a Fortune 50,000 company. Whatever.

When you took this job as a Show Control Engineer you wondered what exciting projects you'd be assigned. So far you've warmed up by sorting the books in the engineering library (twice) and testing the pile of batteries someone found in the bottom drawer of the lab bench. Now you're performing a statistical analysis on the likelihood of beating your PC at solitaire.

Suddenly your big break arrives. Your boss sticks his head through the doorway and says, "Hey! Creative needs someone to sit in on a preliminary meeting for the new Floating Lily Pad attraction, and I've got a three o'clock tee time. Take care of it for me."

It's inspiring the way your boss trusts you like that.

So you trot down the block to the building where the creative people work. You can't help noticing that the carpets are plusher here. Well actually, there are carpets here. Instead of concrete. And this building actually has windows.

In the conference room you settle into the plush chair and fight the impulse to take a nap. A few creative people have already arrived. One of them occupies his time by making a scale model of the Eiffel Tower out of toothpicks and coffee creamer packets.

At last the Project Manager staggers in and you settle down to business. An artist sets some storyboards on an easel and describes the concept of the ride in warm and fuzzy terms. You don't quite catch all the details about metaphysics, but you're pretty sure that antigravity was mentioned more than once. And then there was that part about holograms...

"So," says the Project Manager, turning to you, "how much will that cost?"

"Ummm..."

He waves his hand impatiently. "You show control guys... you never wanna be pinned down." He scribbles something on his pad. "Okay, okay. You can give me the numbers next week."

He turns to an artist at the far end of the table. "So, Jaques, give us the details on the preshow. How's the invisibility part coming along?"

Congratulations. You're a Show Control Engineer.

To get to this point you probably grew up loving theme parks. Someone gave you some good advice along the way and pointed out that most of the technical design in theme parks is done by Electronic Engineers. You probably also studied control systems. And you also know a fair amount about software. To get your engineering degree you had to take courses in Physics, Chemistry, Materials Science, Thermodynamics, and Children's Literature. Well, only kidding about the Kiddy Lit, although it was a fun class.

That breadth is a good thing, because more than any other part of theme park design, Show Control Engineering requires someone with extensive cross-discipline knowledge. You need to be the Jack (or Jill) of all trades.

Your background will serve you in good stead, as you try to decide whether the people around you are intentionally lying to you, unintentionally lying to you, or just don't know what the heck they're talking about.

It will also help you make important decisions like how to control mechanics so they aren't subjected to unnecessary wear, how to design a control system that doesn't require ten years of programming to implement, and how to stay out of the way of moving vehicles or irate Project Managers.

As the Show Control Engineer you are often the peacemaker:

You assure the manic-depressive Audio Engineer that the sound can be dynamically controlled to counter the damage wrought in the studio by the tone-deaf sound designer. "Sure, we'll just fade it as the vehicle passes through the scene."

You soothe the hypertensive Special Effects Designer who has just discovered that if the lava pump is activated for more than two seconds it explodes. "We'll just cycle it intermittently from the show control system, one second at a time."

You save the Set Designer from disgrace. "We'll just stop that periscope before it harpoons the ceiling tiles."

Most of all, you are the great communicator:

You make sure that the audio engineer knows you are controlling his equipment using contact closures, not a battery from a 1947 Packard.

You make sure the contractor pulls UL approved wire, and keeps it away from that Tesla coil in the preshow.

And you make sure the Project Manager knows you need to start testing your system well before opening day. This last request won't do you any good, but it was worth a try. And you can always use the Project Manager to test that Tesla coil.

Chapter 26: Types of Show Control

Perhaps you already have some preconception of what show control systems look like. Maybe a roomful of supercomputers with cables dangling everywhere. Or banks of hamsters in wheels with little bicycle chains running this way and that. Or how about a shaft lined with revolving 78 RPM records, each one carved into unique shapes to control the motions of animated figures?

Believe it or not, one of those actually was the show control system for the original Pirates of the Caribbean attraction at Disneyland. Can you guess which one?

If you guessed the 78 RPM records, you're right. Shaved into cams, their shapes controlled the movements of the animatronics.

Today's show control systems are a bit more complicated than that. The form they take depends upon the function they must perform. But before we describe what they are, let's look at what they aren't.

The Case Against PCs

In general, show control systems are not personal computers. There are several good reasons for this.

At first it seems like a great idea to use PCs for show control. They're easy to get, everyone knows how they work, and they're so cheap these days they're almost a commodity.

But the design life of a theme park attraction is at least seven years. Many are expected to operate for 10 or 20 years. During this entire time they must be maintained. In order to maintain them you must be able to obtain spare parts. Suppose lightning damages part of the show control system. In the middle of the night someone has to diagnose it, find replacement boards, install one, and verify the system works exactly the same way it did before the lightning strike.

Have you ever tried to replace a component in a PC that was several years old? The circuit boards used in today's PCs won't even plug into PCs made more than a few years ago! Besides, a modern PC's motherboard incorporates most of the functions that used to be individual cards. What if the original system simply won't function the same way on newer, faster, different hardware?

Since PCs are certain to change dramatically from year to year, the only solution to this problem is to stock multiple spares at the outset. But this eliminates any price advantage that the PC might have had.

The fact that everyone knows how PCs work also proves to be a disadvantage. Because the maintenance person knows how to configure his home PC, it's a great temptation to reconfigure the one in the show control system. But what works at home may not work in the park.

On one memorable installation I spent nearly an hour trying to debug a system that incorporated a PC, then discovered the maintenance crew had reconfigured it to install a copy of the game "Doom".

So PCs are only used for very specific applications in show control, where the system is largely insensitive to the hardware configuration of the PC itself.

Real Time Show Control

There are two fundamentally different types of show control systems: real time show control and scripted show control. The hardware used in these two types of systems is as different as the applications.

Real time show control systems are used for animatronic and other tightly synchronized shows. They are programmed by artists working at consoles covered with knobs. These "programmers" overdub the animation data in much the same way that a musician lays down tracks for a song. The animatronic figure's elbow is on one track, the shoulder on another, and so on.

Real time show control systems are almost always recorders. They capture the changing data from the knobs on the fly and then reproduce it over and over again until the artist is satisfied with result. They are usually synchronized with SMPTE (Society Of Motion Picture And Television Engineers) timecode in the United States or EBU (European Broadcasting Union) timecode in Europe.

Real time show control systems aren't just for animatronic control. They are also used for many live stage shows, or anywhere that a sequence of events must happen rapidly. They make it easy to tweak the timing interactively.

Live stage shows are one area where PCs are used in show control systems. The most popular systems use the PC to display the status of lighting, audio and controls. But the PC hardware itself is not usually directly involved in the control of any of these. It is simply being used as a graphical user interface (GUI). Should the PC fail, it can probably be replaced by a newer model without affecting the behavior of the show.

Scripted Show Control

Scripted show control systems are used when you need to control the show using... drumroll please... a script.

Remember our theater example? The preshow doors, curtains, house lights, and all the rest? That was a typical application for a scripted show controller.

Scripted show controllers tend to be black boxes that live in equipment racks for decades, silently repeating the same sequence of actions over and over. Most people wouldn't even recognize them as computers, although inside that's what they are.

To those familiar with industrial automation, the scripted show controller may seem a lot like a Programmable Logic Controller (PLC). PLCs are small sequencers that were originally developed to operate automated equipment on assembly lines. The automotive factories in Detroit use millions of them. But PLCs are a poor choice as a show controller. Their programming is based upon timers; trying to use them to implement a script can be a nightmare. We'll discuss PLCs a bit later, though, because they are often used for ride control.

Scripted show controllers are designed so that they can't easily be fiddled with. Once the timing of the show is worked out, the Art Director doesn't want some enterprising maintenance person changing it. There is typically no GUI on a scripted show controller, just a small status display.

But PCs have their role here, too. The PC is usually used as the "front end" for programming scripted show controllers. This is often done with a laptop. Once the programming is done, the PC or laptop is removed, and the black box does all the work.

Scripted show controllers are programmed using a spreadsheet that looks, quite literally, like a script, with show times in the first column and actions to the right. If you'd like to see what the front end for a scripted show controller looks like, you can download a free copy of WinScript from www.alcorn.com.

Chapter 27: You Want Me to Control What?

I haven't actually needed to control any floating lily pads. But the thing that makes a Show Control Engineer's life so interesting is the wide variety of stuff that does need to be controlled.

The weirdest thing I ever had to control was a balcony full of dancing faucets. A major plumbing fixture manufacturer sponsored the show at Epcot's Innoventions.

When somebody asks you to make water faucets dance you can't exactly go to the Yellow Pages and look up "Controllers, Dancing Faucet". Instead, my Mechanical Designer turned his office into what looked like a plumbing supply store. He disassembled them, played with them, weighed them, measured them, took them out on dates

Well, all right, this guy needs to get a life. But you get the idea. He knew everything there was to know about how faucets move. Then he started looking at ways to animate them. He got samples of pneumatic valves, servomotors, stepper motors and solenoids.

"Whoa!" you say, "What is all that stuff?"

We'll cover these things in more detail when we explore mechanical engineering, but here's a quick rundown: pneumatic valves provide a way to turn air on off as it flows through a tube; servomotors are electric motors that can move smoothly to any desired position; stepper motors are motors that step to discrete positions around a circle; and solenoids are little plungers that really hurt if you're sitting on them when they go off.

All of these things can easily be activated by most show control systems. The question was: which one to use?

We mocked up some faucets using all of the different devices and tried them out. Normally an Art Director would be called in to make the decision, but since this was a relatively small project we engineers got to play Art Director. In the end we settled on servomotors for the main movements so that we could accurately control the position of the faucets' "torsos". We used pneumatic valves for smaller, discrete movements. We rejected the stepper motors because they didn't move smoothly, and the solenoids because they were too noisy.

This range of options is typical of the panoply (I've been trying to work that word in for half the book; go look it up) of choices often presented to Show Control Engineers.

Let's look at some of the other stuff we might encounter as we stumble around the construction site that is our themed attraction.

People Counters

Have you ever wondered why the theater hostess always says, "Please move all way to the end of the row, filling every available seat"? It's because she knows exactly how many seats there are in the theater, and she knows how many guests there are in the audience. And they're the same number.

Is the hostess really that good at counting? Or is there some trick involved here?

There is a trick. It's called a People Counter, and it's usually provided by the Show Control Engineer.

As you entered the preshow you passed through a narrow space where an infrared beam counted you. The results are displayed near her podium. As each person enters, the count goes up. The People Counter is pretty clever. It never counts handbags as an extra person, and it even gets most of the children, unless they're plastered to their mother's hip.

Perhaps while you waited for the show a few people decided they would rather catch an early lunch, or skip the show entirely and simply Exit Through Retail. As those people departed, the people counter subtracted them from the total guest count.

When the People Counter reaches the theater capacity, no more guests are allowed into the preshow area. This is accomplished by either a velvet rope or a full body block, depending upon how determined the guests are.

So when those theater entrance doors open, the hostess does indeed know that she has one—and only one—seat available for every guest.

Sometimes the People Counter is tightly integrated with the show system. In Epcot's American Adventure it can control the show cycle time, allowing more "fill/spill" time for heavily attended shows than nearly empty ones (as if there were such a thing!).

Countdown Clocks

Along with the People Counter, nearly every theater show also has a Countdown Clock. A Countdown Clock is a sort of people pacifier. It lets guests know how long it will be until the next show begins, and gives them something to stare at blankly while they stand in the air-conditioned preshow, recovering from heatstroke.

Some Countdown Clocks can be set to different amounts of time, depending upon how often the show is running. Others always start at the same time, but guests are not allowed into the preshow until there is that amount of time left until the next main show.

The challenge for the Show Control Engineer comes when the Countdown Clock must be themed. In simple attractions the Countdown Clock may be nothing more than an LCD timer. But that doesn't fit in too well with old West theming. Or a medieval castle. So if the Art Director wants your countdown clock to be a grandfather clock—or an hourglass—get ready for a challenge. If he wants a sundial, it's time for a new Art Director.

Synchronization

One of the biggest responsibilities of the Show Control Engineer is synchronizing everything in the attraction. Audio must be synchronized to film. Animation must be synchronized to audio. Each scene on a ride may be synchronized to the vehicle motion. Special effects must synchronized with sound effects. And in some rides—

ones conceived by particularly demonic Art Directors—music must run continuously throughout the entire ride, but loop through different lengths in different scenes.

The Show Control Engineer makes all of this work together. He or she typically accomplishes this with elaborate scripts running in a show controller that receives cues from ride vehicles and issues commands to all the other equipment.

The Show Control System is like a giant switchboard, and the Show Control Engineer is a frenzied operator, patching inputs to outputs in response to the demands of a hundred different clients.

Special Effects

The Special Effects Designer really keeps the Show Control Engineer on his or her toes. Special effects incorporate just about any technology you can imagine: mechanics, electronics, high voltage, pneumatics (air), hydraulics (nasty smelling, caustic oil), projection, lighting, and even cryogenics (cold stuff, like liquid nitrogen—don't touch!)

Speaking of cryogenics no, Walt Disney isn't frozen inside of Snow White's castle. There is a basketball court in there, though.

But I digress.

Many of these special effects require local control boxes. A control box is a sort of industrial strength local interface that allows maintenance to service the effect when the attraction isn't operating. For example, a liquid nitrogen effect may incorporate an insulated tank (like a giant thermos) that must be refilled every evening. This can be a complex process, requiring pipes to be purged of air and then pre-chilled so the liquid nitrogen won't evaporate. Safety mechanisms are needed to prevent the maintenance guy from accidentally turning himself into Mr. Freeze.

Such control boxes are usually designed by the Show Control Engineer. They provide local control and monitoring, and often include local safety interlocks. Control boxes usually have a "Hand/ Off/Auto" switch. When the switch is in the "Hand" (or "Manual") position, buttons on the box control the effect. When the switch is in the "Auto" position the main show controller can issue commands. And when the switch is in the "Off" position the effect is disabled.

Pumps

As you ride the boat around Epcot's Land Pavilion you pass through a tropical rain forest where mud flows endlessly down from the high mountains into the Amazon.

It's not easy to move mud. It's thick. It's heavy. It's full of chunks.

The Special Effects Designer tried a lot of different things before he found the perfect solution: a German sausage meat pump.

No, I'm not kidding.

If you can control one of those, you can control anything.

Hot dog!

Chapter 28: Monitoring, Safety and Maintenance

There's more to show control than just control. As you learn the ropes, you'll find it's the extras that make a truly great Show Control Engineer. Here are some of them.

Monitoring

When we talk about Show Control Engineering it's easy to forget that control is only half the job. In nearly every controlled system, monitoring is also needed. That's because the control signals that move stuff, turn on lights, play audio, or trigger effects all expect a response.

Any well-designed show control system makes sure this response occurs. If it doesn't, the show controller takes one or more actions:

Shuts down the controlled equipment if there's any likelihood of damage.

Notifies Maintenance that the equipment needs to be serviced.

Activates alternate or backup equipment, if available.

The better-designed systems respond quite intelligently to such problems as they arise.

In a well-designed theme park, show controllers in individual attractions collect this information and relay it to a central monitoring point such as Epcot Central, or Legoland's administrative offices.

Pressure Mats, Etc.

There's nothing that ruins a theme park engineer's day quite like squishing a guest. And it's amazing what lengths some guests will go to in order to get squished. Standing up on a roller coaster? Climbing out of a log boat while shooting through a flume? Crawling over the lap bar and jumping between vehicles? These don't sound like good ideas to me. But you'd be amazed how many guests will try them.

A lot of these unsafe activities fall in the domain of the Ride Control Engineer. (A few of them are governed only by God.) But the Show Control Engineer also tries to lengthen the lives of guests foolish enough to tangle with moving equipment.

If you climb out of a ride, chances are good that you'll step onto a pressure mat. The show control system will sense this and deactivate all action equipment in the area. In all likelihood the ride system will also shut down. And a lot of disappointed guests will stare angrily at you.

Break beams can also provide a measure of safety. If the guest climbs out of the queue area and into a space with moving set pieces, he's likely to break an infrared beam on the way. This will deactivate the set pieces and cause burly uniformed men to reunite him with his mother.

When the topography is too complicated for pressure mats, digital imaging techniques can be used. Video surveillance systems are now sophisticated enough that they can sense motion in portions of the picture where there should be none. If something moves where it shouldn't, the show control system shuts things down.

Things That Go Boom

The Show Control Engineer must sometimes control things that explode.

Explode intentionally, I mean.

What would a stunt show be without a few spectacular explosions? Most stunt shows involve pyrotechnics (fireworks), natural gas or propane, and big things that fall down. And, of course, it's not exciting unless there's an actor nearby.

Most stunt shows are only semi-automated. A Technical Director sits at the front of the audience, firing the effects as the stunt performers do the show. But Technical Directors aren't perfect. The stunt performers get very annoyed if the Technical Director sets them on fire. Stunt performers may be accustomed to having their eyebrows singed off, but they're rather fond of their major extremities.

So the Show Control Engineer comes to the Technical Director's rescue, and interposes a level of safety between the Technical Director's finger and that giant gas explosion.

For these applications the Show Control Engineer must design something more like a ride control system than a show control system. Fault tolerance, redundancy, and other Ride control techniques are used, and the system must be subjected to a complete Failure Modes and Effects Analysis. These topics will be discussed soon.

Design for Maintenance

If it ain't broke, don't fix it. But if it is broke, it better be fixable in one night.

Theme parks hate having inoperable attractions. So Mean Time Between Failure (MTBF) and Mean Time To Repair (MTTR) are important topics. The Show Control Engineer can help, by designing systems that are easy to diagnose and easy to repair. A well-designed show control system includes status displays that report problems, and special diagnostic modes that test the equipment, either automatically or manually.

As a Show Control Engineer, if you design a system like that you'll be the maintenance guys' best buddy. They might even take you out for a beer.

But if your system just sits there when it's broken, without giving a hint as to the cause..., well do you see that bucket of tar and feathers over there...?

Chapter 29: Alone in the Dark

It's been eighteen months since your boss called you into that meeting about the floating lily pads. Somewhere along the way the lily pads turned into a simulator ride. And the invisibility effect in the preshow took a major hit at a budget meeting and ended up being a video monitor.

But throughout it all, your boss stood by you. Well, actually he was standing on the fourteenth tee, but he had a cell phone with him.

Now it's four o'clock in the morning on opening day. In just a little over four hours hundreds of happy people will be enjoying the attraction you worked so hard to create.

Or not.

Contrary to every project schedule ever printed, your test and adjust time didn't begin two weeks ago. It started at eight o'clock last night. That was when the electricians finally got everything hooked up, and the painters moved enough stuff out of the way that you could at long last get to your show control cabinet.

Now you're sitting on the floor of the preshow area, your laptop tethered to the show control cabinet with a two-hundred-foot-long cord that snakes down the hall and through three doorways.

The building smells of concrete dust and new carpet. You squint under the harsh glare of the worklights. It's eerily quiet. Quieter than it's been during all the noisy months of construction.

Only the Ride Control Engineer remains, probably to make sure you don't break anything. The construction crew is gone. The technicians are gone. Even the Project Manager is gone, back to his hotel room to catch a few hours of sleep before the grand opening. You find that pretty amazing, considering he's never seen the whole attraction run.

At the outset he had very little confidence in you. But over the long months he's watched you as you've coordinated your activities with others on the project. He's watched you bring your equipment in under budget. He's observed your calm demeanor throughout (not realizing it was due to your having no idea how much trouble you were in until this very moment).

Now, he's put his fate in your hands. He's gone home and left the attraction to you.

Your fingers are shaking a bit as you make one final change to your show control script. Perhaps it was that seventeenth cup of coffee.

You nod at the Ride control engineer. He arms the system.

Your mouse hovers over the download button. Did you remember all your changes? You leaf through your notes, but it's hard to read between the hydraulic oil stains.

What the heck. You click download.

The work lights turn off. The lighting ramps to daytime operating level. The preshow entry doors close. Unfortunately they close on your laptop cable, dragging it several feet across the floor, but at least they closed.

The preshow monitor comes to life and you watch the preload briefing, which was funny the first 600 times you saw it.

"Come on", you mutter. You watch the simulator entrance doors, silently willing them to open.

And they...

... open. Right on cue.

The load music continues inside the vehicle, then the doors close and you hear the ride start. A moment later the preshow doors open for the next group.

The group that will be the first to experience your new attraction.

Congratulations.

Now you really are a Show Control Engineer.

In our next chapter we'll see if you've got what it takes to be a Ride Control Engineer. Until then please refrain from eating, drinking and smoking while on the ride.

You'd just get it all over yourself, anyway.

Chapter 30: The Ride Control Engineer

Q: Who is the first passenger on a theme park ride?
A: A sandbag.

There are a number of reasons for this. Sandbags have very low health insurance costs. Sandbags look better wearing shorts than the average theme park guest. And sandbags can't sue you.

Now we'll discover why all of those characteristics are important in the world of the Ride Control Engineer.

The coffee was bitter, and his hand was sweaty as he set the cup down next to the control panel. It had been a long day, and a frustrating one. It seemed for every line of code that he wrote he had to delete two others. Then there had been power problems, and some of the wiring needed to be reworked.

Now it was late, and he should be heading home, but the imperative was upon him. If he didn't get this working soon, they might put someone else on the job.

It seemed simple enough.

There was a rotating turntable. It turned at a constant speed, regardless of what happened on the track. It had walls that divided it into five segments. Around the circumference the ends of the walls hung out over the track.

Which meant the walls could run into the vehicles.

What he had to do was keep the train from hitting the walls when it inserted itself into a segment of the turntable.

It seemed simple enough.

But the turntable couldn't stop. And it weighed a lot.

More than a lot. About one million pounds.

Not a good thing to hit a train with.

He sighed. The sensors on the train would tell him where it was. And the encoder on the turntable would tell him where it was. So it was just a matter of hurrying the train into the turntable as the wall passed, and staying close to that wall as the wall behind came along.

Then, three-fourths of the way around the turntable, the track bent away from it and he was freed of the pressure of trying to stay ahead of that inexorably moving wall.

The train sat in the station. It had been hours since he'd had the guts to try it. The last time the darned thing had barely moved before an Emergency Stop had shut it down.

Normally E-Stops were good. They guaranteed safety. But if one happened while the train was entering the turntable, and the turntable couldn't stop in time...

He drained the rest of his coffee, set the cup where he wouldn't knock it over, and flipped on the power to the track. A light he'd hung on the front of the train showed it was energized. The turntable began to rotate, its walls sweeping across the curve of the track in the semi darkness.

Sweaty fingers on the keyboard enabled the Ride Control Computer. The train lurched, stopped, then smoothly accelerated out of the station. No E-Stop this time. Good. Within a few feet it settled into a conservative speed, passing a corral where a plastic horse grazed on plastic grass.

The turntable was up ahead. The train slowed as it approached, trying to synchronize with the inexorable rotation of the walls. The train curved around the Feed Store and nosed closer to the wall, slowing and accelerating, hunting. The wall swept across the track just ahead of it, and the train accelerated, trying to hug the wall's trailing edge.

Too close. The front of the train bumped the wall, and the impact caused it to brake. The ride control system interpreted the stutter as a "Following Error", and activated the Emergency Stop.

The train stopped.

But the train was only halfway into the turntable, and the turntable was still turning. In dismay the Ride Control Engineer watched as the next wall rotated out across the track, catching the train's midsection and sweeping it from the rails, dragging it across the terrain, dragging the Feed Store into the pasture of plastic grass. The plastic horse fell over.

The Ride Control Engineer sighed. He reached over, picked up the train and set it back in the station, aligning the wheels with the track.

Two months, he thought. Two months from now and that would have been the real thing.

He picked up his coffee cup, then set it down again. Maybe the coffee would be better in the morning. He switched off the lights as he stepped out of the lab.

Chapter 31: All Things That Move

What do Ride Control Engineers control? That might seem like a silly question, but the answer may be more diverse than you anticipate.

Vehicles

Of course they control vehicles. But just as there are many different types of vehicles, there are many different ways of controlling them. Some require far more sophisticated control systems than others. And some require far more safety analysis.

The easiest types of vehicles to control are ones that don't go very fast. Boat rides, for example.

Most boat rides are propelled simply by the motion of water around the Ride. Pumps aimed in the direction of travel maintain a constant flow, and the boats... well, they go with the flow.

With most boat rides it doesn't even matter if one boat bumps into another one, with one exception. It's very dangerous for boats to collide in the load and unload area. This can knock down people who are standing. To prevent this there is generally a "boat stop" just before the unload area.. It prevents boats from entering the unload area when there's already one there. Other boats back up around the Ride, and the boat stop lets one boat at time advance so the passengers can disembark.

Add a waterfall to your boat ride (the kind of waterfall the boats go down, not the kind that goes into the boats) and things start to get complicated. Now you need a boat stop at the top of the waterfall to make sure the boat can't rush down the waterfall and collide with a slow-moving boat at the bottom.

Add enough boat stops and enough monitoring and you've got what is known as a "block zone" control system. In a block zone control system the ride is divided into zones. These zones may be short or long. The smallest possible zone is at least as long as your vehicle—a boat in this case.

In a block zone system, a zone is considered occupied if there is a vehicle in it, and unoccupied when there's no vehicle. In order to guarantee that no vehicle can ever hit another, there must always be at least one unoccupied zone between any two occupied ones. A control mechanism—a boat stop, or simply turning off the propulsion system in a powered vehicle—stops any vehicle at the zone boundary until the zone ahead is unoccupied.

Block zone systems may be used in rides as simple as a boat ride, or as complex as a bobsled ride. (A bobsled ride is one like the Disneyland's Matterhorn or Space Mountain, with individual, high-speed vehicles moving independently around a track, all at the same time.)

While it might seem pretty simple to control a boat ride, it's often even simpler to control a ride—even a high-speed ride—that has only one vehicle. Surprisingly, roller coasters fall into this category. On a roller coaster, only some rudimentary speed control and the ability to stop the roller coaster in the unload area are required. Beyond that, what goes up... must come down.

Another easy type of ride to control is an Omnimover. These are rides like the Disneyland's Haunted Mansion where all of the vehicles are attached to a single moving chain. Obviously vehicles cannot hit one another. In a way, there is only one vehicle; it's just very long.

Some rides are entirely controlled manually. A steam train is an example of this sort of ride. Usually attractions such as these don't even need Ride Control Engineers.

On the flip side, there are rides that go nowhere but require complex Ride Control Engineering. Simulators, for example, are extremely complex to control.

Most safety issues with simulators relate to the movement of guests—not the ride platforms. A sudden movement of the simulator during load or unload could injure guests. The ride system must hold the simulator in a quiescent state while guests are exiting or entering. This includes any elevators used to position ramps at the entrance and exit. Any movement of the simulator while the elevators are in place could cause serious damage.

During the ride, multiple sensors ensure each guest remains secured in his or her seat. Any "escape" will cause an Emergency Stop.

(One alarming story details the adventures of a guest who chose not to leave the exit ramp of a simulator before the exit doors closed. As the elevated ramp retracted he found himself in an uncomfortably small space through which the simulator violently swooped for five minutes as he cowered in terror. I'm not sure if this is an illustration that well-trained operations personnel are the ultimate safety system, or that there should have been pressure mats on the ramp. Or perhaps it's just evolution by natural selection.)

And More

Q: When is a stage show a ride?

A: When there are so many safety systems that it can no longer easily be controlled by a show control system. (In the trade this is known as a "Shride".)

This is the case in Epcot's American Adventure. No guest has ever ridden one of the stage hydraulic lifts up and down—I hope—but there are so many potential collisions between stages and building, props and building, or stages and other stages that a ride control system was needed to monitor for failures that could lead to equipment damage.

There are many more examples of attractions on which no one is intended to ride but which require extensive safety analysis and the most reliable control systems. One example is Pyro. Pyrotechnics. You know, fireworks.

What would a stunt show be without a few explosions? And while a tank full of propane and a spark create a lovely fireball, there's nothing quite like real fireworks to make an audience duck. The design of a safe Pyro system requires extensive safety analysis and some very special engineering. Even the electrical grounding of the wires is important when working with Pyro.

In one memorable incident, a seemingly innocuous change in the way wires were routed at a stunt show in Las Vegas—a change that involved no alteration of the electrical circuit whatsoever—resulted in the unintentional detonation of fireworks when stunt personnel were standing nearby. It caused serious injuries.

Even two-way radios are not allowed around Pyro. The radio waves can set off the sensitive explosives.

Synchronization

The Ride Control Engineer sometimes forgets that what he's working on will ultimately be judged by its show quality. While most of the show system design is the responsibility of the Show Control Engineer, it's often the job of the Ride Control Engineer to make sure that the ride is synchronized to an already playing show. This sometimes means tight integration of the ride control system and the show control system. Nine times out of ten this pain in the neck is left to the Show Control Engineer. But some problems can only be solved by careful attention to ride control.

Chapter 32: Safety

If there's one single thing that distinguishes Ride Control Engineers from all of the other engineers who work on theme parks, it's safety. Ride Control Engineers live, breathe, and eat safety. They talk about safety with their friends when they go out to lunch. They talk about safety with their families on the weekend. They talk about safety when they're playing golf. Now that I think about it, Ride Control Engineers can be really tedious.

But if you meet a Ride Control Engineer who's not concerned about safety, run the other direction as fast as you can. Because when you get onto a theme park ride, you put yourself in the Ride Control Engineer's sweaty hands.

There are many ways the Ride Control Engineer guarantees your safety. He has many tools of his disposal. This chapter presents just a few of the elements that Ride Control Engineers use to make your trip a safe one.

Computers vs. PLCs

Do you have a PC?

Of course you do.

Has it ever crashed?

If you said "no" with a straight face, you'd make a good politician (or you own a Mac).

So how would you like to be on a ride that depended upon your PC for its safety system?

Me neither.

That's why PCs don't make very good ride control computers. And yet you see them all the time, connected to simulators, monitoring safety systems, cycling vehicles. How is that possible?

We said that PCs made poor show control systems. But do you remember where PCs were useful in show control? One of the spots was for operator interface: status displays, statistics, cycle times, and so on.

PCs find their use in ride control systems in many of the same functions. They're good at displaying a lot of information in a small amount of space and allowing the user to tailor that information to their needs. But PCs are also used to do the actual control function of some rides.

Is this just foolhardy? Well, in some cases, yes. Simple attractions such as mall-based simulators are often controlled by a single PC. The reasoning is that if the PC fails the simulator will stop. And if the PC goes nuts, it can always be unplugged.

R-i-i-i-ght.

This sounds very logical at first, but it is actually a fairly flawed piece of thinking. I've seen simulator setups where a single failure of the PC output could cause the simulator to jump several feet. During the load or unload cycle this could be extremely hazardous.

A true Ride Control Engineer wouldn't do this, and you won't find such a system in a theme park.

Theme parks tend to use PLCs (Programmable Logic Controllers) for ride controllers. PLCs are industrial controllers designed for factory automation. They are comprised of extremely reliable hardware, but can be difficult to program, because they are primarily intended for simple automation tasks such as running a canning line. Nevertheless, they are the controller of choice for most attractions.

Still, you say, I want to use a PC. Well, there is a way the PCs are used in ride control to directly control rides.

The incentive is simple. PCs are cheap and fast. They're easy to program. So they provide the most straightforward way to control complex new attractions.

As long as we find a way to make them safe. Here's how:

Redundancy & Voting

Redundancy means more than one of something. If something has a one in a million chance of failing, it's regarded as fairly dangerous in theme parks. This may surprise you, but in a theme park it doesn't take long for something to happen one million times. Particularly if it's happening several times a minute.

If we now take two of those something's and require them both to agree for the action to take place, we'd like to believe that the chances of failure are now on the order of one million times one million. Unfortunately, that proves to be wishful thinking for most failure modes.

For example, if the failure is due to an error in our software, and the same software is loaded into both computers, then the chances of failure are still exactly the same as with one computer!

On the other hand, if the failure is a hardware failure (or a software failure caused by some hardware failure such as a memory fault) then using two computers does increase our reliability.

The simplest way he to use redundant computers is to insist that the two computers agree at all times. If the computers ever disagree, then the system shuts down.

This technique works great for systems where shutting down is always safe. But it doesn't solve the problem in a system where shutting down the computers is, in itself, a dangerous thing to do. In systems like these we need to use yet another computer.

By using three computers to control a ride, we can create an extremely robust environment. For the ride to operate normally, all three computers must agree. If one of the computers disagrees, the two remaining computers are assumed to be correct. (The chances of the two computers agreeing and being wrong are about 1 in a gazillion unless the software is extremely poorly written.)

The advantage of using three computers is that when one disagrees, the other two can bring the ride to a safe shutdown while ignoring the odd man out. This means that trains can complete their ride cycles, and the guests be returned to the unload station. This is much safer than bringing the ride to an immediate stop and evacuating guests from it. (Ride spaces are not easy to walk through, and not all guests are physically able to navigate the evacuation routes, so this is a far safer solution.)

Triple redundant computer systems are only used in the most advanced rides, because they are expensive. But they're an ideal solution for dangerous rides when absolute safety is required.

Single and Multiple Point Failures

Ride Control Engineers spend more of their time analyzing the ride control system than they do designing it. The major thing they're looking for are failure points.

A failure point is anything in the system—hardware, software, mechanics—that if broken will cause an unsafe situation.

There are four general types of failures:

- Single Point, Undetectable—This type of failure, when it occurs, is catastrophic. Imagine the brake pedal falling off of your car; You wouldn't notice until you tried to step on the brake, and then it would be too late.
- Single Point, Detectable—Catastrophe can sometimes, but not always be averted in the case of this type of failure. Suppose there is a warning light that indicates the brake pedal has fallen off. It only helps you if you aren't in imminent need of the brakes.
- Multiple Point, Undetectable—Catastrophe can sometimes, but not always be averted in the case of this type of failure. Suppose there are two brake pedals. If one falls off you might have time to use the other one. But what if the other one fell off undetected last month?
- Multiple Point, Detectable—This is the only acceptable type of failure. Suppose there are two brake pedals and two warning lights. If one pedal falls off, you know that you should use the other one to stop the car at a service station and get it fixed.

It's easy to identify failure points in a system. It's much more difficult to correct them. Here's a simple example:

Suppose you have a gravity ride such as a bobsled ride. The vehicles are stopped in the station by an air brake. The brake is activated by an electronic output. If the brake is not applied, the vehicle can crash into the rear of the preceding vehicle, leading to an unsafe situation, injury, bad press, lawsuits, and general unpleasantness.

How can the brake fail?

It can fail mechanically: perhaps one-half of it falls off. It can fail pneumatically: the air hose falls off. It can fail electronically: the output fails to activate. It can fail in software: the computer fails to turn it on.

How can we make this system safe? Let's try this:

The maintenance staff inspects the brake every evening to make sure that it isn't damaged. They also inspect the hose to make sure it's securely attached and not cracked. Because they cannot inspect the electronic output we decide to add a second one. If either of the outputs comes on, the brake will be activated. Finally, we test our software under all known conditions to make sure it always activates the brake at the correct time.

Does that all sounds reasonable?

In fact, it's a disaster waiting to happen.

The fact that the brake is undamaged in the middle of the night says nothing about its condition by the next afternoon. The same applies to the air hose. And the fact that our software worked perfectly during test doesn't mean a thing. What if it's somehow altered, either intentionally or unintentionally?

Worst of all is the idea of adding a second electronic output in parallel with the first. This is what is known in the trade as a "multiple point undetectable failure". That's a big no-no.

Suppose one of the outputs fails. How would we know?

We wouldn't.

Which means we're now back in exactly the same situation we were when we had only a single output. In short, two outputs are no better than a single output from a safety standpoint. Unless the outputs are monitored.

If we monitor the outputs, things get much better. Now, when the first output fails, we immediately know that we're only one more failure away from an unsafe system. This allows us to unload the ride using our remaining output, and then repair the failed one before we load any new guests.

Similar monitoring could ensure that air pressure was always available at the pneumatic hose. But that doesn't solve our pneumatic problem. The pneumatic actuator itself may still fail to apply the brake. To improve the safety of pneumatic brakes, they require air pressure to RELEASE, not to BRAKE.

But this still doesn't fix our problem. Because the air valve may fail in the on position, causing the brake to be commanded to be released all the time.

In fact there is only one solution to this pneumatic problem and the associated mechanical problem of a damaged brake:

Take a good look at the track in the load area the next time you board a gravity ride. There are two separate brakes.

Cycle Testing

Why don't the two brakes have the same problem that the two electronic outputs had?

The answer is: cycle testing. Each time the brakes are applied, each is tested to make sure it mechanically closes on the vehicle. If it doesn't the failure is handled the same way the failure of the electronic output was handled. The ride is brought to a stop gracefully until repairs can be made.

(Notice that the entire foregoing discussion of safety relates to rides with multiple vehicles. This whole category of safety concerns disappears for rides with a single vehicle. Now you see why there are so many roller coasters with a single train.)

Cycle testing finds application in other areas, too. It is the only technique that can validate a safety mechanism that is not normally used.

Suppose there is a track switch on our gravity ride. A track switch directs vehicles around the ride or into the maintenance area. The ride can only be operated normally if the track switch is in the position that directs vehicles around the ride. This is determined using a sensor. But what if this sensor is stuck on?

This sensor must be cycle tested. We must validate not only that it goes on when we command the track switch into the normal position, but also that it goes off when we command the track switch into the maintenance position. Seeing this transition guarantees that the sensor works, every time we move the track.

Break Beams

Break beams are another staple of Ride Control Engineering. They're particularly useful on boat rides for detecting the position of the boats. As with other sensors, they must be cycle tested. And on boat rides they must be located so that splashing water does not interfere with their functionality.

Brake beams are also useful for identifying situations that aren't supposed to happen: vehicles moving out of the ride envelope, for example. Unfortunately at this point it's somewhat like closing the barn doors after the horse has already escaped. Still, it's better for the system to know of the failure and shut down what it can, rather than continue to operate oblivious to the problem.

Video Surveillance

Video surveillance is another barn door technique. Around most theme park rides are infrared cameras. (And yes, they can see you necking, even in the dark.) Somewhere a ride operator is watching several monitors, each usually with a four-way split screen display. These show him the activity of guests all around the ride. And while he may enjoy watching you neck, he definitely won't be amused by your standing up. Speakers throughout the ride allow him to issue warnings; if guests don't comply he can shut down the ride. It's a long walk to the exit amidst the glares of your fellow passengers.

Pressure Mats

Pressure mats are reserved for the real idiots: the guy who manages to get completely out of the ride vehicle. Anyone who's ever seen the chains and gear and rotating tires that make theme park rides go has trouble imagining who would be stupid enough to do this. But people do. The pressure mats are a last-ditch attempt to shut down the ride before the guest pays a visit to that giant meat grinder in the sky.

Murphy's Law

Murphy's law says, "Anything that can go wrong will go wrong."

In Ride Control Engineering, "Anything that can go wrong will go wrong if we let it. But we can't let it."

So the life of the Ride Control Engineer is one of constant vigilance—and fairly high stress. But just so that you don't get the idea that there is no fun in Ride Control Engineering, let's take a brief look at the fun you can have with water pumps.

The Norway boat ride at Epcot Center is designed so that water pumped from a reservoir in the basement circulates from the top of the ride down through a trough. The boats are lifted to the top of the trough with a chain drive and then float down.

It's important that this water keep flowing. It important for two reasons.

One is that without water boats don't float.

But an even bigger reason is: the reservoir won't hold all the water.

It's sort of like juggling chainsaws: it's easier to keep them going around than it is to catch them.

Of course, there are electrically activated "weir" dams around the ride that are designed to hold back the water if the pumps stop. These can be tricky too, though. One day as I drove up to the building there was a lovely waterfall flowing out of the third floor emergency exit door.

And if the control system fails to raise the dams when the pumps stop...

Well, let's just say that more than once we tested how much water the gift shop would hold.

To Exit Through Retail that day would have required a rowboat.

Chapter 33: How To Get Free Beer

As with any well-engineered system, ride control systems must be designed to facilitate maintenance. Broken ride systems are notoriously difficult to diagnose, and any help the control people can provide is greatly appreciated by the maintenance department.

This means, at a minimum, the ride control system should be able to self-diagnose all of its own activators and sensors. This ability can be provided through test procedures that allow maintenance people to display the status of the sensors as they walk around the track, manually activating them, and a screen from which they can manually cycle each activator while someone with a radio checks them in the field.

Ideally the ride control system should also support mechanical maintenance of the system, allowing motors to be exercised, and monitoring temperature, oil, water, and air systems.

Here are just a few of the maintenance functions that we provided for Universal Studios Earthquake train:

The train can be positioned at any point along the track

The hydraulic pumps can be manually activated.

Each of the three cars can be individually manipulated using manual controls to raise and lower the lifting pistons, either individually or together.

Communications between the train and the master control computer are continuously monitored and errors are logged.

The temperature and pressure of oil in the reservoirs of each car are monitored and logged.

The responsiveness of the hydraulics system is monitored. If it doesn't accurately follow our commands, we display a warning message. This helps catch degrading components before they cause a real problem.

A heartbeat signal between the show control system and the ride control system allows the ride control computer to make sure that the show system is operating.

The entire E-Stop (Emergency Stop) system is self-tested every time the ride is brought out of E-Stop into run mode.

All of the track position sensors are cycle tested.

The track position sensors are individually identified and the order in which they are expected (for both directions of travel) is monitored. If the sensor is missed the ride shuts down.

The ability of the system to kill the main power is tested every time the main power is first applied.

It's easy to spot Ride Control Engineers who've spent a lot of time in the field. They're the ones with easily diagnosable systems. They're also the ones the maintenance guys take out for beer after work.

Chapter 34: Kisses in the Dark

It was dark in the building. I could hear the turntable walls whisk past, but otherwise one million pounds of black beast in a black hole moved silently past me, a giant lumbering inexorably by in the dark.

Motors in the track hummed as the shiny blue train approached, hesitating, trying to pace the approach of the next wall. It seemed almost afraid to advance.

The glare of overhead show lighting blinded me, so that I could hardly gauge the train's position. Judging the position of the next evil wall was even more difficult.

"Can you see it?" I called. On the other side of the track the programmer and the maintenance lead shook their heads. It was too dark.

My sweaty palm nervously caressed the E-Stop button. We'd tested the turntable E-Stop again, and the stopping distance was no better. If the vehicle got behind, there was no way to avoid damage to it or the track. So the E-Stop would only work during the first part of the vehicle's insertion. After that...

The hum of the motors increased as the vehicle surged passed me, diving into the black doorway of the turntable entrance. I watched the sandbag passengers glide past, fat blobs of burlap sprawled across the seats.

The vehicle nosed in behind the trailing edge of the turntable wall. Was it close enough? I shined my flashlight into the black hole but could see nothing.

The vehicle lagged, dangerously I thought, then lurched forward again. What the heck was it doing? My hand hovered over the E-Stop button. But the vehicle was past the point of no return. Even if I pushed it, the turntable wouldn't stop in time.

I could see the next wall approaching, inexorable, gigantic. Half of the last car still protruded from the doorway.

With a surge like the last duckling in a line, afraid it would lose its mother, the car lunged ahead and tucked itself into the gap. A second later the turntable wall swung past and kissed the car's bumper.

We'd done it.

A week later the attraction opened to guests.

**

Now you know what it means to be a Ride Control Engineer, from lonely nights in the lab to the last terrifying moments when the mad doctor breathes life into his experiment.

Next we'll look at the far more relaxed world of the audio/video engineer.

Until then...

...well, you'd better keep your finger on that E-Stop button.

Chapter 35: The A/V Engineer

The theater is blissfully silent.

The acousticians have done their job well. The air conditioning is a mere whisper of a breeze wafting through the subconscious.

It is time to "equalize" the theater—a time that A/V Engineers live for. A time when the thousands of dollars spent on sound processing equipment are at his beck and call, to raise or lower the sound pressure level of each narrow band of frequencies until the audio source is reproduced in the theater space exactly as it sounded in the recording studio.

In mid-theater the A/V Engineer hovers over his sound mixing board, a bewildering collection of multi-colored LEDs, motorized sliders and really expensive black buttons, all quite intimidating to the uninitiated.

The A/V Engineer rubs his hands together, then presses one of the really expensive black buttons. The theater suddenly is filled with noise. Mind numbing, drive you insane, static. Niagara Falls.

A few lingering construction workers jam their hands over their ears and run for the exit, along with the entire scenic design crew and a small family of rats.

The A/V engineer hums tunelessly to himself and smiles.

It's playtime.

He points his sound pressure meter at nothing in particular, presses the trigger and examines the result. "Hmmm Down 6dB at 10KHz."

He tweaks a knob. Niagara turns into four o'clock in the morning television static.

He smiles happily and takes another reading.

Outside the rats are burrowing into the planter.

"Pink" Noise

This cacophony is called white noise, and it's one of the A/V Engineer's most valuable tools. White noise is comprised of all of the audio frequencies from low bass to high treble, combined in equal amounts. By playing white noise from the audio source and adjusting the sound processing equipment in the theater until all frequencies are represented equally, the A/V Engineer can assure that the audio reproduction system is "colorless". This means it won't alter the sound from the way that it was originally recorded.

The A/V Engineer also uses pink noise. It's another type of test material, comprised of only the lower frequencies without the more annoying hiss. And finally he will use test tones that sound a bit like a single note played on a flute.

With enough knobs at his disposal, it sounds like a fairly straightforward task to set the audio in the theater to be colorless. But there are problems.

The theater is probably an unusual shape, and has many different surfaces that reflect sound. There are probably dozens of speakers around it, some of which only will reproduce a limited range of frequencies. And the Show Producer and Media Designer have probably thought of a hundred changes since they left the recording studio. So getting the audio response right in every single spot in the theater is... well, impossible.

In fact, the job of adjusting the audio is very subjective, and there are probably as many different opinions on the best settings as there are A/V Engineers on the job.

Some theme parks do the actual audio mix in the theater. This means the master material is actually altered to fit the acoustic performance of the theater, and rerecorded to incorporate these adjustments. If everything goes perfectly, the tone controls for the theater will end up set absolutely flat. Did I just say, "If everything goes perfectly"? Heh, heh, heh

There was a time when theme park audio was expected to be pretty poor. Of course, there was also a time when if you weren't near the stage at a rock concert you couldn't tell what band was playing.

The public's expectations for audio quality in public spaces increased dramatically during the 1970s. By the time that Epcot Center opened in 1982, theme park audio was among the best anywhere. Now if they could just do something about the hamburgers.

Of course, even at Epcot the audio quality differed from pavilion to pavilion. The better-designed theaters could reproduce the sound of a violin so accurately it might bring tears to your eyes, while in a noisy ride the audio on-board the vehicle still might be barely intelligible. But things have continued to improve since then. Every year theme park audio becomes more integral to the overall experience.

Super Black and Retrograde Technology

Theme park video has followed a somewhat different trajectory. There was very little video in theme parks at all during the 1970s. But with the invention of the laserdisc player, video took off. Although laserdiscs never caught on in the consumer marketplace, they were a staple in theme parks for almost 20 years. By the early 1980s most theme parks were loaded with videos, and the quality was excellent. Laserdiscs could freeze the picture perfectly, search almost instantly, and play material at different speeds or even backwards. They were very easy to control, as they consisted of a series of up to 65,000 pictures, each of which could be called at a moment's notice.

Since then there has been little improvement in the quality of video. In some ways the quality of video has even deteriorated. Here's why:

With the advent of DVD and Blu-Ray players, laserdiscs went the way of the dial telephone. But most modern video sources use digital video formats such as MPEG-2 to compress the data into a size that can be stored on today's media. While these are useful formats for home video, they have serious limitations in theme park use.

Digital video sources lack many of the capabilities of laserdisc players. On many, not every frame is accessible. Usually video is stored in a few enormous files, rather than as thousands of individual pictures. Trying to jump to a specific picture is like looking for a needle in a barrel of nails.

And material doesn't necessarily play smoothly at slow speeds, or backward at all.

Digital video sources are also incapable of playing "super black", a level of black so dark it's impossible to tell whether the monitor is even turned on. Super Black was very useful, because it allowed monitors to be concealed when they weren't in use. With today's video sources other techniques must be found.

The fact that thirty years later we're still struggling to do things we could easily accomplish with laserdiscs is a testament to their original design.

Chapter 36: Audio

The A/V Engineer has finished his adjustments in the theater. The massive mixing board covered with expensive knobs has been put back into storage. Any remaining audio adjustments must be made using the tone controls in the equipment room. It used to be that these were rows of knobs or sliders on equalizers. But these days most of the audio processing chain is done with digital signal processors – computers that let you draw virtual control panels on-screen and modify the audio in just about any way you can imagine.

Now the "golden ears" crew has arrived. These are guys with the reputation of having such finely tuned listing abilities that they can detect the tiniest shade of difference between sounds. (You may be wondering how to acquire such a reputation. The first step is to spend a year's salary on your home stereo. Or better yet, just on the speakers.)

Sound levels are measured in decibels, or dB. It's a sliding scale, so that even a quiet room has about 50 dB of background noise, yet 120 dB is so loud that it can cause hearing damage. The golden ears guys adjust the sound by listening in the theater, then radioing changes in decibel levels to the A/V Engineer in the equipment room.

One of the "golden ears" crew is in the theater now, calling in adjustments on his two-way radio. The A/V Engineer is sitting at a table in the equipment room, with his radio by his elbow. He's eating a sandwich.

"Take down the center channel 2 dB," comes the instruction over the radio.

"OK," says the A/V Engineer into the radio. He takes another bit of his sandwich.

After a minute the radio crackles to life again. "Now bring just the bottom end of the center channel back up 1 dB."

The A/V Engineer sips his coffee, picks up the radio and says, "Check."

There's a long pause, and then the radio says, "OK, now bring up the surround channels 2 dB."

The A/V Engineer finishes his sandwich, tosses the wrapper into the trashcan, picks up the radio and says, "Gotcha."

The Show Control Engineer is fiddling with one of the I/O racks. She turns to the A/V Engineer and says, "Wow, he must really have educated ears to make such fine adjustments."

"Yeah," says the A/V Engineer.

"How are you making those adjustments, anyway?" she asks.

"I'm not," he says, taking another sip of his coffee.

"Huh?"

"He'll have everything back just the way it started in another thirty minutes anyway, so why bother?" The A/V Engineer heads for the restroom. He takes his radio with him.

Audio Sources

There was a time when almost every audio source in a theme park used magnetic tape. Those days are gone. Now the audio sources have almost no moving parts. Sounds are stored in memory or on a hard disk and played back digitally.

In the days of magnetic tape, there were three distinctly different types of player for the three major audio applications: multitrack shows, triggered sounds, and background music.

Multitrack shows used magnetic tape with as many as 24 channels of audio playing in a continuous loop. These would be used for theatrical shows, and also for rides, where each channel of audio went to a different area. An example is Disneyland's Pirates of the Caribbean, where the underlying musical score runs synchronously throughout the attraction.

Triggered playback for sounds along a ride track was provided by "Cart" machines similar to the ones used in radio stations. Their tape cartridges contained a short loop which was triggered to play once each time the track sensor was triggered.

Background music (BGM) was sourced from long reels of conventional stereo tape that were automatically rewound and restarted upon reaching the end.

Technology now allows all of these applications to be handled by a single digital audio system. The best of these systems are capable of accommodating all three different types of requirements—at the same time—out of the same unit. We'll discuss modern digital audio players in more detail in the maintenance chapter.

Signal Processing

In a perfect world we wouldn't need to process signals. They'd emerge from the audio player exactly the way we needed them, be amplified and distributed to speakers. But in the real world things don't always sound the same in the theater or ride space as they did in the sound studio. Signal processing equipment allows the A/V Engineer to tweak things until they're just right.

Until recently nearly all signal processing consisted of rows of knobs or sliders that performed parametric or graphical equalization. Those are fancy sounding words for essentially a giant tone control.

The problem with knobs is that well-intentioned maintenance people can readjust the audio characteristics they don't like the way it sounds. This tend to annoy A/V Engineers who've spent weeks adjusting things just the way they want them. So a form of equalizer was developed that had no knobs or sliders. It was programmed using a computer. Once the computer was removed voila! No fiddling allowed.

In the past few years there has been an almost wholesale move to digital signal processors (DSPs). DSP's are specialized computers that are very fast at mathematical operations. They treat all audio as a series of numbers, and can manipulate those numbers in whatever way they are programmed. This means that a single DSP is able to adjust the bass, treble and other frequency bands, and add delay, reverb, echo or even noise filtering.

This is extremely useful equipment to place in the audio distribution chain, because it allows nearly any contingency to be handled. Without DSPs, all sorts of other specialized equipment— such as switchers, delay generators, noise filters, or limiters—might be needed in order to get the show space to sound right. The DSP can play all these roles, without taking up extra rack space or adding cost.

Perhaps you've adjusted your home or car stereo for one song, and then found it didn't sound as good on another song. The same sort of thing can happen in a theme park. So digital signal processors are not only programmable, their programming can be changed "on the fly". This means that the show control system can send commands to the digital signal processor to adjust any characteristic of the sound at any time during show.

Some of the signal processing requirements in a show are similar to those you might encounter at home. Others aren't. For example, your home probably doesn't have any rooms that are 200 feet long. (If it does, you might want to consider opening a bowling alley.) But 200 feet is a modest sized space in a theme park.

Why does the size of the space matter? Amazingly, it's because of the speed of sound.

In everyday life we tend to assume that things like light and sound travel from one spot to another instantaneously. This is actually a pretty good assumption for light. Unless you're trying to hold a conversation with astronauts on the moon, you're not aware of the delay that occurs over long distances for things—such as radio waves—that travel at the speed of light.

But sound is a lot slower than light. We use this fact all the time to measure how far away lightning is. We know that it takes about five seconds for sound to travel a mile, so by counting the time between seeing the lightning and hearing the thunder we can gauge the distance.

It turns out that even in a relatively small space—such as a 200 foot long theater—it takes a significant amount of time for sound to travel from the front to the rear. About one-fourth of a second, in fact. That doesn't sound like very much, but if you see someone's lips moving and then hear what they're saying, completely out of sync, it's quite annoying.

This effect can partially be eliminated by synchronizing the sound to the film for a seat exactly in the center of the theater. That way in a 200 ft. theater no one hears the sound off by more than 1/8 of a second. But that still can be annoying. It becomes an even bigger problem in larger theaters.

I recall a visit to the Hollywood Bowl where we sat in the "nosebleed" seats. I wouldn't say these were lousy seats, but I needed binoculars just to see the ground. At the beginning of the show the pianist (it was Marvin Hamlish, but who remembers him?) dramatically raised his arms above the piano and brought them crashing down to form the first majestic chord of music. Except we didn't hear anything. For a lo-o-o-o-ng time. I was afraid that by the time we heard the end of the song, Marvin Hamlish's career would be over. It was a close call.

In a theme park—or even your neighborhood Cineplex—this effect is compensated for by distributing the sound to different parts of the theater at different times. The sound is actually played back before the action occurs on the screen. Speakers aimed at people farthest away reproduce the sound first. The sound that goes to speakers near the audience is delayed. The result is that everyone hears the soundtrack more or less in synchronization with the images.

Patch Panels

Patch panels are rows of holes into which cords can be plugged to connect the sound through the audio system in different ways. They are extremely handy for checking out or isolating different parts of a system. Patch panels are usually designed so that they pass the audio through the normal path when nothing is plugged in; the cords are used only to make modifications.

With the advent of DSPs, patch panels are no longer particularly useful, since the audio can be dynamically rerouted right inside the computer. In fact the most modern theme park audio processing cabinets couldn't use a patch panel because the sound is never an analog signal.

What?

That's right, from the time it's retrieved from memory or hard disk to the time it's delivered to the amplifiers, the sound in modern audio processing cabinets is never anything but a sequence of numbers. All of the digital processing is done entirely... well, digitally. A single cable can carry 24 channels of this audio from the source to the DSP and a second cable distributes it to the amplifiers.

Amplification

Once they have the sound modified just the way we want it, we need to make it a lot louder. The signals that roam around in the audio processing cabinet are tiny. It takes a lot more to drive the speakers in the theater.

This increase is accomplished exactly the same way as in your home or car: with amplifiers. But theme parks use a lot more amplifiers that you have in your home or car unless you drive one of those cars that pulls up next to me at the intersection throbbing so loud I have to readjust my rear view mirror.

It's not uncommon for a large theater in a theme park to require thousands of watts of amplification. (In this book I explain what's what, but not what's a watt.) Also, the amplifiers used in theme parks tend to be extremely high quality. After all, once we spend all that time and money getting the sound just the way we want it, we're not likely to scrimp on the power bill.

Speakers

There are as many types of speakers as there are confused customers milling around in neighborhood stereo stores. And that's a bunch. There are woofers, tweeters, electrostatics, horns, drivers, Venturi ports, bass reflex systems... you get the idea. Whatever I say about speakers will be obsolete in two minutes and disagreed with by half of the A/V Engineers on any given attraction anyway. Suffice it to say that the ultimate goal of the attraction's speakers is to deliver undistorted sound to every guest.

There are two basic techniques for distributing sound to speakers. You're familiar with one from your home stereo. Using this technique the amplifiers expect to see a particular load on each audio channel.

This load is measured in resistance, and expressed in Ohms. Your home speakers are probably eight Ohms, and your home amplifier is assigned to drive either 4 or 8 Ohms on each of its outputs.

Most theme park speakers work this way as well. But there's another type of distribution used in theme parks and other public places, including your neighborhood shopping mall or department store. It's called 70-volt audio distribution. Those flat, round speakers you see mounted to ceiling tiles usually use this scheme.

70-volt audio distribution requires a transformer on the amplifier output, and another one at each speaker. You might wonder why anyone would want to go to the trouble of using a system that requires so many extra parts. The reason is that using a 70-volt distribution system we can hook many speakers a single amplifier output, and with very cheap wire. And the contractor can wire the speakers in the ceiling willy-nilly. And with some contractors, willy-nilly is as good as it gets.

While 70-volt speaker systems are perfectly adequate for most background music applications, they don't provide sufficient volume or audio quality for theaters.

Synchronization and Control

If there is anyone on the Theme Park Design team who is most concerned about synchronization, it's the A/V Engineer. We've already mentioned the pains that he takes to assure that the sound is synchronized with the film or video image. He also needs to make sure that sounds are synchronized with visual effects, and that triggered sounds on a ride are played back at the dramatically correct moment.

This means the A/V Engineer probably spends as much or more time working with control systems as he does working on audio distribution. It's not uncommon for the audio system to contain a control system completely independent—and cued by—the show control system. Particularly if we include programming the DSP, A/V Engineers are progressively becoming more and more technocentric.

In most installations the A/V Engineer is also responsible for sourcing industry-standard timecode that locks all the other parts of the show or ride together. This is called SMPTE (Society of Motion Picture and Television Engineers) timecode in the U.S. and EBU (European Broadcast Union) timecode in Europe. It consists of a stream of bits, played at audio frequencies, which uniquely identify every frame of the show. (A frame is about 1/30th of a second in the U.S. and 1/25th of a second elsewhere.)

This timecode is distributed to the show control system, the lighting system, and sometimes the ride system. It identifies every moment of the show cycle uniquely.

PA

No, this is not a hillbilly's father. It stands for Public Address, another of the A/V Engineer's responsibilities. Most themed attractions have PA stations throughout the ride. These can page into individual areas or throughout the entire attraction. The system is generally integrated with a park-wide PA system as well. These days the PA system is usually controlled by the DSP. It sounds simple at first, but the system must be able to interpret any one of a hundred buttons and route the live audio from that mike to the preassigned areas associated with that button while allowing prerecorded audio to continue playing in other areas. Think of those annoying "Now boarding rows 25 and higher only" pages at Gate 73 and you get the idea.

In some themed attractions the A/V Engineer also installs intercom systems at the Operator Control Consoles so that the operators can make dates with each other between shows.

Chapter 37: Video

"The executives are coming in for a test show," the Show Control Engineer said.

"Not another dog and pony show?" the A/V Engineer asked.

"Yup."

The A/V Engineer sighed. "Well at least we're ready for them. There won't be any disasters like last week."

"Yeah" said the Show Control Engineer, dubiously.

"Hey, what could go wrong?"

"Ahh, here they come now. Get ready."

"What do you mean get ready? I don't need to do anything. I'll just be glad when they're done, so I can get back to work." The A/V Engineer leaned casually back against the equipment rack. He watched the Show Control Engineer start the show, just as he felt his shoulder press against the eject button on the video player.

Video Sources

As audio sources have migrated from tape to digital storage, so too have video sources. Nearly all new theme parks are equipped with digital video players that use either memory or hard disks for media storage.

Like audio systems, where most of the audio is distributed digitally, video is also migrating to all-digital systems, although high bit rates make this more challenging. Video signals may be distributed in several different forms:

Composite video is the least expensive and lowest quality distribution method. It was designed in the 1940s for ease of broadcast, and the color features were added as an afterthought.

Y-C separates the brightness and color signals to achieve a clearer picture. The consumer version is called S-Video.

Component video distributes the red, green and blue signals individually, along with separate sync signals. VGA monitors used a version of this. It produces the highest quality analog picture, but is more expensive.

HDMI is a digital distribution format popular with consumers. Because of cable length limitations it isn't always a good choice in large installations.

SDI is a professional serial digital format used for standard definition video. It is the highest quality video distribution system, but is quite expensive.

HD-SDI is the high definition version of SDI. It the best (and most expensive) video distribution format available. It's also called SMPTE-292M.

Video Formats

Standard definition video in the United States is called NTSC (National Television Standards Committee, although some say it stands for Never The Same Color). In most of the rest of the world it's PAL. PAL stands for... heck, I don't know. Everyone just calls it PAL. Anyway, PAL images are higher quality, but tend to flicker because of a lower frame rate.

The quality of both these video formats is rather appalling in today's computer savvy world. Their resolution is about the same as that of a 1985 vintage 640 x 480 VGA monitor. Yuck.

More and more theme parks and other dedicated venues are using high-definition (HD) video. There are many different resolutions of high-definition video, but the most popular home standard is called 1080i. This produces a picture 1920 pixels wide by 1080 lines high.

The "i" in 1080i stands for interlaced. It means that the picture is drawn as two separate fields that are interleaved, sort of like weaving your fingers together. Interleaved signals are easier to transmit, but can look blurry.

There's a competing format called 720p (the "p" stands for progressive) that doesn't have this problem, but it has fewer pixels on the screen. The different broadcast networks in the United States have adopted competing standards, leading to considerable confusion. But it gives the A/V Engineers something to argue about when they go out for beers.

While it is difficult to quantify the difference in quality between high-definition and standard definition video, simple math will tell you that the picture is about seven times as good. It's also far more suitable for projection.

Unfortunately, the high-definition standards were developed for broadcast use, where frequency spectrum costs money. So the standards committee elected to severely compress the video signal in order to save bandwidth. The result is a picture that is not as sharp as it could be. Theme parks installing high-definition video players usually select equipment that operates at many times the broadcast frequency. They also use resolutions far beyond the standards. The Simpsons attraction at Universal Studios Orlando has over 8,000 lines of resolution!

Video Encoding

Because the high-definition video standards—and standard definition digital video players, for that matter—use compression, the video must be encoded after it is shot, before it can be loaded into the video player. This encoding process is a mathematical operation that reduces the high bandwidth of the original signal to a lower bandwidth series of numbers that will fit into memory or on a hard drive.

Encoding can be tricky. It's an extra step between editing and installation that doesn't always go smoothly (as anyone who's been stuck in an attraction at 2 AM with bad media will attest). As technology improves the process should get easier, though. We keep hoping, anyway.

Video Distribution

Just as audio signals must be amplified before going to speakers, video signals traveling more than a few feet must be amplified, particularly if they are feeding more than one monitor. Video signals don't require the dramatic amplification of audio signals, but video distribution amplifiers (VDAs) are used in nearly all cases.

Video Monitoring

A well-designed video processing cabinet in the equipment room will provide a local monitor, so that the output of the video players can be checked without walking into the show space. A single video monitor with either a switcher or patch panel will handle many video sources.

Displays

The big screen monitor that looks so huge in your living room seems a lot smaller in a preshow area. Theme parks need large displays, and lots of them. These days 60-inch and higher displays are common in themed attractions.

Projection

Video projection is also popular, and improving monthly.

The financial advantages of video projection are overwhelming. There are no moving parts to wear out, and no megabuck film prints that need to be reordered every few months.

One area that remains expensive, though, is bulbs. Most people have no idea how expensive a projector bulb is—whether for video or film projection. A typical projector bulb lasts only a few weeks in a theme park, and they cost several thousand dollars! And a single fingerprint can cause them to explode—violently.

Better have someone else change it.

Chapter 38: Keep It Sounding Good

Video and audio maintainability have improved dramatically in the last few years.

Most theme parks now use hard disk or memory-based video playback devices such as the Digital Video Machine. These devices have far fewer moving parts than a disc player. This means that their life is much longer. While disc players might only last a few years or less in a theme park, digital video players have a design life of ten years or more.

Another advantage of these digital video sources is they don't gather dust. Dust settling on the surface of a DVD or Blu-Ray disc can make it impossible for the player to find the video. So theme parks have to dust every disc every month. This might not sound like a big deal, but at Walt Disney World there were once hundreds (if not thousands) of these players. That represented a major maintenance cost.

Audio players have also improved. When Epcot Center opened in 1982, Epcot Central—the centralized control and A/V distribution facility—was filled with tape binloop machines. Each of these machines was the size of a washing machine. In the top were hundreds of feet of magnetic tape, each striped with 24 tracks of audio. The tape formed an endless loop that repeated all day long. An air pump minimized friction and kept the seemingly random wad of tape from snagging as it squirmed its way around. Every night the machines were laboriously disassembled and the top surface polished with Turtle Wax. Talk about maintenance intensive!

Back in 1982 background music was sourced from large reels of quarter inch tape. And triggered sounds were on tape cartridges.

And all of these tapes wore out. Regularly. So every few months new tapes were copied from the masters and loaded into the machines. Hundreds of machines.

Advancing technology obsoleted these tape devices. Products like the Alcorn McBride Digital Binloop store audio on flash memory. There are no moving parts.

The washing machines have been replaced by cages of circuit cards smaller than a breadbox. And the cost of maintenance has been reduced to nothing. The Mean Time Between Failure (MTBF) of this new equipment is measured not in days or months, but in decades.

Chapter 39: Heard Any Good Ones Lately?

Installing audio and video systems in a theme park can be a lot of fun. But it can also be frustrating. It's not all tweaking knobs and buying expensive speakers. The A/V Engineer is involved in the project almost from the start. He has to understand how the spaces are going to be used in order to design systems that can accommodate their requirements.

As with other types of electronic engineering, the design of the audio and video system has a large impact on the facility, even before the building is constructed.

Audio and video systems generally require separate power from show control, ride control and other equipment. This is to prevent hum and other noise from migrating into the sound and picture. This separate power is brought all the way from the transformers outside the building. It is essential the ground of the circuit be independent. In equipment rooms these special electrical outlets are often colored orange to signify they have an isolated ground.

At the Pro Football Hall of Fame in Canton, Ohio we spent a week trying to identify the source of hum in the audio system. Finally, after disassembling half the audio gear, we discovered that the supposedly isolated ground was actually shorted to the normal ground outside the building.

Another way the A/V Engineer must be involved in the early design of the building is to specify conduit runs. Conduit—as anyone who watches the Three Stooges knows—are pipes full of wires. These pipes route signals from the equipment room to the show space. Many must pass through concrete, so it's vital to know where they're needed before construction begins.

Audio and video signals require big conduit. You know how thick one piece of coax for your TV is. Distributing a single component video feed requires five of those coaxes! Just imagine if there are a dozen monitors in the preshow area. Conduit is one area where size does matter.

***

In this chapter we've looked at the rather fun world of audio / video engineering for theme parks. If you like to tinker with home hi-fi systems; if you buy imported CDs because you think the plastic is purer; if you won't let your spouse hold the remote control it might be your dream job.

On the other hand, if you'd rather just tell your spouse what channel you want to watch, maybe you're management material. Coming up, we'll tour our attraction prior to opening day, and interview many of the other engineers—including managers—who've worked so hard towards opening day.

Until then...

...Shhhhhh. The audience is listening.

Chapter 40: Into the Void

For a year or two we've shepherded our project from blue sky through design, culminating in the electronic engineering disciplines of Show, Ride, and A/V Engineering.

Now our designs are complete, our equipment fabricated. It's been shipped to the field and installed. Hopefully in the right place and not connected to 480 Volts.

Meanwhile the construction crews have nearly completed the building. It has power, and air-conditioning, and thousands of cables snaking their way through miniature labyrinths of conduit.

Finally the big moment has arrived. Every resource we can bring to bear must head for the field as we plunge into the turbulent sea of test and adjust.

We'll meet the other members of the technical team as they struggle to ready the attraction for opening day.

Coordination

It looked like a big tuna can in the middle of a sand box.

It was easy to explain the sand. They hadn't yet paved the plaza in front of the pavilion. Epcot's opening was still weeks away, so what was the rush?

The tuna can was harder to understand. On the drawings it had looked futuristic, cutting edge even. But the drawings always showed the view from high above. Maybe they were for visiting seagulls. But standing below the fifty-foot-tall cylinder of stainless steel panels it looked just like well, a giant tuna can.

At the front there was an opening, where the ride track emerged from the lower level, circled a massive column, then plunged back into the building at the upper level. The vehicles, stopped now, were a shiny blue in the late afternoon sun.

The Coordinator walked alongside them, up the track, looking for the Project Manager, who'd asked him to meet in Scene One.

For two years he'd coordinated every little detail of the construction of World of Motion. He'd made sure the scenery designers knew how wide the ride vehicles would swing on the turns, made sure the painters would be out before the programmers arrived, and kept the lighting designer from strangling the architect when the latter had refused to allow trusses into the site lines of the guests.

Now they were getting down to the last days. It sounded apocalyptic. With only weeks before the preview shows, tempers were short and competition for resources was fierce.

It was his job to keep everyone talking, and make sure they had what they needed, whether it was a cherry picker for installing lighting fixtures, or a bushel of hamburgers to keep the carpenters working overtime.

A section of the walkway was missing up ahead, so he squeezed between the vehicles, crossing to the other side of the track and continued upward.

Architectural, Structural and Civil Engineering

At the transition from the Florida afternoon's warm humidity to the cold dry air conditioning the architect stood with Disney's construction manager and the construction company's foreman. Above them, where the two atmospheres collided, water condensed from the lower lip of the stainless steel cladding, splashed onto the deck next to the ride vehicles, and ran down the entrance ramp. The foreman had unrolled a sheaf of blueprints and balanced it on the railing. His look said, "We built it just the way you designed it, friends." Well, maybe not friends.

The Coordinator had already sat in a two-hour meeting about the exterior treatments, and was pretty sure that in there they'd already decided to spend more money, and would need a rush order of something-or-other to reroute the deluge.

For now, everybody seemed to be communicating, so until they needed him he could focus on other things. He slipped past them, into the cool darkness of Scene One.

Project Management

The Project Manager was watching one of the Scenic Artists work on the backlit footprints embedded in the cave wall. There were over 100 of these lighting effects, each mounted in their own can, and attached to the rear side of the fake cave surface. The idea was that the footprints would be invisible until they were illuminated. Activated in sequence, it would look like someone walking up the cave wall and into the ride.

But the first attempt to disguise the footprints had been pretty clumsy, so now they were coming back and over-painting, trying to blend the backlights into the surrounding rock surface.

But it wasn't paint that was on the Project Manager's mind today. He wanted the Coordinator to schedule a meeting of the technical staff to discuss when the building could be turned over to Maintenance and Operations for training.

"And make sure everybody shows up," he said. "I don't want anybody claiming they didn't know."

He nodded, but didn't say anything. With all this construction it was hard to imagine the engineers ever being ready to turn over the attraction.

The Project Manager was interrupted by his call sign on the radio. "Project Seven bye," he said into it, and waited for the message from Central Base. These days the traffic on the radio was nearly continuous, but after a while you didn't even hear it anymore, until your call sign came through. Then some subconscious reflex snapped you to attention.

"10-4. Seven clear," he said, and slipped the radio back onto his belt.

The Coordinator noted the time of the meeting by writing it on his palm with a ballpoint, then followed the ride track into the building, looking for members of the technical team.

Chapter 41: Lighting and Effects

In the central part of the building, the ride track circled around a large expanse of blackness. Far below him was a swirling sea of eerie clouds. Emerging from this roiling fog bank were miniature skyscrapers, swathed in an unearthly blue glow. Tiny vehicles seemed to glow in the dark as they traversed the spaces between the skyscrapers.

Standing in the midst of this miniature city, the Special Effects Designer struggled to get a tiny hovercraft back onto its track. Off to one side, the Lighting Designer experimented with different colored gels for the lighting fixtures. The Special Effects Designer turned pink, then green, then back to blue.

Lighting

Lighting is a combination of artistic and technical endeavor. The selection of fixtures, colors, placement, and transitions all come straight from the theater.

Not the theme park theater. I'm talking about Broadway.

Many theme park lighting designers have worked on Broadway, and most would say that the artistic design portion of their job is what they like to do best. But there's no question there's a technical component to the job, and far more so than on the stage.

That's because the average theme park attraction lasts a lot longer than the average stage production, and probably has a much higher budget. Some of that money is spent on making sure the lighting system will be both robust and economical to maintain.

Lighting designers in theme parks also have the luxury of a year or two of design time, rather than the tightly compressed schedules found in most stage productions. They are also free from the weight and size restrictions that restrain traveling productions, and aren't limited by the capabilities of an existing facility.

That's the big difference. Theme Park Lighting Designers usually have input into the physical design of the spaces they are to light, the location of structures to hold their lighting fixtures, and the amount of power available to feed them. This absence of constraints means that doing lighting design for theme parks can be a lot of fun.

On the other hand, Theme Park Lighting Designers must do the most important part of their job—the field work—in the same incredibly compressed schedule that confronts the other engineering disciplines. This means long nights just before opening day, and competing with the construction trades and other engineers for access to the facility.

We all know a little bit about lighting, because we've all changed a light bulb at one time or another. Or stuck our finger in a light socket. So we can imagine some of the challenges that Lighting Designers face: wattage requirements, heat dissipation, electrical code requirements. These details must be worked out years before the attraction opens, but so far it seems pretty familiar. But there are differences.

In your house a switch controls most of your lighting. We flip a switch and electricity is connected to the light bulb. It comes on at full brightness. End of story.

Very little of the lighting in a theme park attraction is controlled that way—often only the fluorescent worklights that come on when the park is closed.

In your dining room perhaps you have a dimmer switch that lets you adjust the brightness of the chandelier over your dining table—for those romantic dinner for two. Or so people can't see the crayon marks on the wall.

The lighting in our themed attraction is controlled using a computerized version of that dimmer switch. Nearly all of the fixtures are fed by dimmer cabinets located in an electrical equipment room (EER). These dimmer cabinets are fed by a serious amount of power from electrical distribution panels, rout it through computer-controlled dimmers (each of which is capable of illuminating your entire house) and send the dimmed voltage to the various fixtures.

There may be close to one hundred channels of dimming in a single cabinet, with each channel individually controlled. The dimmer channels are rated in kilowatts. Values of 1 to 4 kilowatts per channel are common. (A kilowatt is enough power to control at least a dozen of your bedside lamps, so we're talking about some serious power here.) We're also talking about some serious fans for cooling.

The dimmer cabinets are controlled by some sort of lighting controller. The lighting controller is, in turn, cued by the show control system. After all, the show control system knows what time it is in the show loop, and is coordinating the audio and ride, so it may as well handle lighting, too.

The lighting controller is often a lighting board, although this is an expensive choice. Lighting designers like to use a lighting board during test and adjust, because it allows them to tweak each fixture to the perfect brightness. So the lighting board often becomes a permanent part of the installation. But a better way to design the lighting control system is to transfer the settings from the lighting board into a dedicated piece of equipment designed for permanent installations. This prevents the settings from being fiddled with later.

The connection between the lighting controller and the Dimmer cabinets is usually a signal called the DMX (DMX stand for Digital Multiplex, which means a bunch of digital values interleaved). It sends the values of 512 different lighting channels continuously, updated many times per second.

The DMX signal can connect to multiple Dimmer cabinets. The only limitation is the 512 channels. If more than 512 channels are needed, an additional DMX "universe" is added.

Some modern lighting has a computer-controlled dimmer built right into the fixture. In this case the DMX signal is routed around the field, to the actual fixtures.

There are a few types of lighting that are difficult or impossible to dim. Florescent lighting is notoriously problematical. Although not much conventional florescent lighting is used in theme parks, a specialized form of it called ultraviolet or "black light" is. "Black lights" make florescent paint glow spectacularly in the dark. There are few themed attractions that don't make some use of this technique.

Most "black lights" can't be connected to dimmer cabinets, and must be turned on in the morning, and off in the evening. This is still done by computers, through a computer-controlled switch.

Perhaps you've seen moving spotlights at a rock concert. These fixtures are complex to control, usually requiring multiple channels of DMX. Different channels control the brightness, the color, and the motion of the fixture.

Most fixtures are far simpler than this. They throw a specified amount of light a known distance at a known angle. If the light needs to be colored, a filter called a gel is placed in front of the bulb. Think colored cellophane.

Normal filters fade quickly in continuous use, like red printing fades if you leave it in the sun. To avoid the constant maintenance costs of replacing the filters, theme parks use special, very expensive filters, called dichroic glass, or dichroics. These glass filters are custom-made to produce a specific color. Conventional gels are used during test and adjust to determine the perfect combination of colors, then the dichroics are ordered to replace them.

Another way that Lighting Designers minimize maintenance costs is by treating the fixtures gently. If the bulb is designed to accept 110 volts, no more than, say, 100 volts is ever sent to it. And the dimmers never snap the full voltage on all at once. Even for quick changes they do a slight ramp. This combination of "derating" and ramping dramatically lengthens bulb life.

You can try this at home. My father-in-law grew tired of constantly replacing his porch light. So he took two light bulbs and wired them in series. This resulted in each light bulb operating off of half its normal voltage. Of course the bulbs were dimmer than normal; but there were two of them. As far as I know, those bulbs are still working today. And he did this in the 1950s. The light bulb makers don't want you to know this trick! (A word of warning: if you don't know what you're doing, electricity-wise, don't try this at home. Electricity can permanently cancel your ticket.)

Special Effects

Fog is a staple of the Special Effects Designer. Its swirls about mysteriously, masking the sins of the Set Designer. It also creates a fluid surface for the Lighting Designer to play with. And it looks cool.

Theme park fog comes in a couple of varieties. The most popular is atomized water droplets. In other words, real fog. It's created by releasing water onto rapidly vibrating metal plates, which break it into tiny droplets that hang in the air just like the real thing. The advantage of this water-based fog is it's clean and harmless. The disadvantage is it makes your attraction mildew.

Another disadvantage of water-based fog is that it takes a while for it to build up. It's not suitable for attractions were a sudden cloud is needed in a short burst.

For these applications liquid nitrogen (LN2) is used. When released into the air, LN2 is so cold it instantly vaporizes, creating a dense white cloud of condensation that quickly dissipates. This sudden burst of fog is useful to mask the secret workings of attractions. For example, at Universal Studios a blast of LN2 disguises the ascent of the Back To The Future vehicle into the domed theater.

Air is seventy percent nitrogen, so liquid nitrogen—as long as it doesn't get on you—seems fairly harmless. And it is. But a problem occurs when a lot of LN2 is released in a confined space. The nitrogen can easily displace the air, and before you know it you're breathing an atmosphere containing no oxygen. Thud.

There's nothing like an unconscious guest to give an attraction a bad reputation. So attractions that use a lot of liquid nitrogen incorporate nitrogen sensors, to make sure the air remains... well, air-like.

Another popular tool of the Special Effects Designer is projection —often not conventional film projection, but rather "still" projection. Well, not completely still. These projectors incorporate a moving wheel or film loop. They create the impression of continuous motion. That's an extremely useful way to expand the rear wall of the attraction into the infinite. Spacious skies, amber fields of waving grain, purple mountains caressed by majestic clouds, you get the idea. When projected onto a painted scrim from the rear they're also used for smaller effects, such as burning torches or shimmering seas.

The Special Effects Designer's bag of tricks is about the size of Rhode Island, and we don't have time to empty it all out. So I'll just mention one more favorite: smell cannons. These are devices that release a small amount of scent, usually triggered by the passing of a ride vehicle. Popular scents include hot rocks, roses, and stinkbugs. (Than last one is at Animal Kingdom's "A Bug's Life", in case you want to bring a clothespin for your nose.)

Chapter 42: Nuts and Bolts

The Coordinator continued his journey around the ride.

The doors to the vehicle maintenance area stood open. Actually, he'd never seen them closed.

The transition from the carefully designed show lighting to the harsh florescent lighting in the garage-like environment was jarring.

Mechanical Engineering

The Mechanical Engineer was in the maintenance pit below the track, working underneath one of the vehicles. An assortment of wrenches lay around him. A maintenance technician squatted nearby, watching him work.

"Get me some quarter twenties," said the mechanical engineer. He spoke with a German accent.

The maintenance guy rose and walked to the workbench. The wall above it was covered with plastic bin boxes. He opened one, extracted a number of nuts, and returned.

"This time we'll put some Loctite on them, like they should have done in the first place," said the Mechanical Engineer.

The ride was his baby. He'd designed and drawn every bit of it, down to the nuts he was reattaching. It was an Omnimover, a continuous chain of vehicles that ran around the entire ride. Cams could rotate the vehicles to face the guests in any direction, depending upon where the action was in each scene.

This ride wasn't his first outing with an Omnimover, by any means. He'd used this same mechanism for Haunted Mansion, and helped develop the original version for the long-defunct Journey Into Inner Space at Disneyland. They'd patented that one.

So this installation had gone smoothly. A few manufacturing issues, a couple of tweaks, and he'd be done. Which was a good thing, because he had a completely new and elaborate hydraulic design to debug over in American Adventure, and it was running behind schedule.

When the Mechanical Engineer crawled out from under the vehicle the Coordinator delivered the message about the meeting, then headed back to the ride track.

In the next scene, behind one of the set pieces, was a door labeled EER. He opened it and stepped into the electronic equipment room.

Systems Engineering

Rows and rows of equipment cabinets stretched away from him. Although he didn't know what each of them did, he knew them all by name. He'd worked hard to get every one of them assembled on time, delivered to the field, staged, hoisted through the second floor doorway in the side of the tuna can, maneuvered into place, and terminated. Show control, ride control, audio, video, lighting: he'd made sure they were all here and ready when they were needed.

He found the Systems Engineer standing in front of the monitor cabinet, trying to figure out why the low-pressure sensor on the hydraulic pumps wasn't working. The Coordinator wasn't exactly sure what the System Engineers did. He knew he hadn't built any of these cabinets, but he seemed to know little bit about all of them. Now that he was in the field, he seemed to hang around all the other engineers, so he figured he should be at the meeting.

One time, when he'd asked, The Systems Engineer had told him he "made sure everything worked together." The systems, he meant.

"Guess that makes me a systems person, too," thought the Coordinator. "I make sure everyone works together."

He delivered his message, then headed back out to the ride track.

Chapter 43: Details, Details

He hadn't noticed the squirrels in the picnic scene before. One of them was holding a cookie it had stolen from the picnic basket.

"That's not the way a squirrel holds a cookie," he thought. Oh well, too late now.

Up around the bend was the big city scene.

Planning & Scheduling

A turn of the century horse, frightened by a motorcar, had overturned a cart full of chickens. Their crates were scattered across the intersection, their heads poking out in confusion. Chaos reigned.

Except the moment was frozen in time.

Nothing moved, while the Costumers worked on the animated figures, tugging garments this way and that, adjusting wigs and sleeve lengths. It could be dangerous to work around those animated figures. They were full of powerful hydraulics. So the animation system was completely shut down while they dressed the figures.

An animator sat on the back of the cart, swinging his legs impatiently and checking his watch every minute. The Planner spoke with him in quiet tones, taking notes on her clipboard. He'd been scheduled into this time slot, but he couldn't work without the figures turned on, and the costumers were behind schedule because the painters had been in the way during their time slot that morning, and the painters were behind schedule because the ride was being tested all night, and the ride was behind schedule because the building hadn't been ready...

And on and on.

From the very beginning of the project the Planner had tracked every discipline, following their needs and establishing the linkages between each task and the deliverable that preceded it. She'd used Gantt charts to keep track of everything.

The Gantt chart was a long strip of paper—several feet of it—with a horizontal time line that could be days, or weeks, or even hours, depending upon the need. Parallel lines for each task were drawn between starting and ending points, with milestones shown as triangles.

Notes indicated which tasks needed to be completed before others could start. If one task stretched, it could force dozens of others to slide further down the timeline. Sometimes the chart could also be used to figure man loading, which helped the finance people calculate budget.

Now that they were down to the last weeks, the tasks had become so fluid, that the charts were no longer much help, and the Planner was shooting from the hip. She kept notes of who needed what from whom, and spent her days much like the Coordinator, trying to improve communications.

The Coordinator delivered his message to the Planner and the Animator (who said he was too busy to attend) and headed for the attraction exit.

Safety and ADA Compliance

In the unload area he found the Safety Engineer. He had a steel tape and was measuring the clearance between the moving sidewalk and the railing at the end of unload.

When World of Motion was built, safety hadn't taken on the significance it now holds, but it certainly was taken seriously. The emergency stop system on the ride would be formally tested before opening, and any mechanical pinch points identified and protected.

The Americans with Disabilities Act (ADA) was still a decade away, but Epcot already provided handicapped access to most rides, and infrared transmitters that beamed audio to special receivers carried by the hearing impaired. The system was also used to deliver foreign language versions of the show and ride narration to overseas visitors.

The Coordinator delivered his message and headed out of the building.

Technical Writing

He found the technical writer in his corner in the Cast Services Building. The door said Women's Locker Room, but the place was filled with desks and chairs. In another few months it would be filled with women in marching band costumes, Chinese outfits, or spacesuits.

The Technical Writer had a sheaf of blueprints unrolled on his desk, and was copying notes onto a yellow pad. Next to him, a two-foot-high stack of notebooks balanced precariously.

The Coordinator sometimes suspected the Technical Writer knew less about the equipment in the attraction than he did. But he certainly turned out thick documents. He wondered if anyone would ever really read the manuals that the Technical Writer was writing.

He delivered the message, then went to his office in one of the construction trailers.

Finance

He checked his watch. Lunch was over in California. He picked up the phone and dialed. The finance guy answered on the first ring. No, he wouldn't conference call during the meeting. He'd just get an update about the schedule tomorrow, from the Coordinator.

He seemed anxious for them to turn the building over to Operations. Something about billing numbers, and whose budget was charged for incidentals after the handoff.

After he hung up the Coordinator checked his watch again, then realized he'd just done that. There was still time to drive out to the warehouse and see if those missing parts had shown up. He grabbed his radio and headed for the parking lot.

Later that night he pulled his car up in front of the construction trailer. It was dark, but still hot and humid as he unloaded several cardboard boxes of hamburgers and soft drinks. Bugs swarmed around the mercury vapor light of the parking lot.

Inside, the meeting was about to begin. He distributed the food and the settled into a chair in the corner with his yellow pad, ready to take notes.

Another day on the site was behind him; there was one less day before opening.

He looked at the tired and anxious faces around him, and thought, "What an incredible collection of people, each willing to work so hard to accomplish so much."

He felt proud to be a part of it. And determined to keep them working together—for at least a few weeks more.

Chapter 44: 102

World of Motion opened—went 102 in Disney jargon—for a special preview to construction workers and their families on Labor Day weekend, a full month before the opening of Epcot Center. It was one of the few attractions open that day, and certainly the most complex. Its flawless opening and exceptional operating record were a testament to the talents of the many men and women who created it.

With over one hundred animated figures, it was the largest attraction of its type ever created. World of Motion was a perennial favorite with guests for more than a decade.

But as with all themed attractions, the old has to make way for the new. Guests—or in this case the sponsor—wanted something fresh and exciting. In a world of MTV and shoot em up videos games, nuance gives way to action. And so World of Motion closed at the end of 1995, to eventually be replaced by Test Track, a high-speed ride through well, a tuna can.

***

We've seen the culmination of our efforts. From Blue Sky through Installation, we've created an attraction and brought it to life. Our reward is watching the delighted guests as they emerge from our work. And reading some good reviews in the newspaper and national newsmagazines.

And a long nap.

But it takes more than one attraction to make a theme park. In fact, it takes more than a collection of compelling attractions to make a theme park. We need to provide guests with a complete experience from the moment they enter the parking lot. This experience must include landscaping, signage, food service, shopping, and entertainment.

Creating an entire theme park is almost like building a city. We'll need infrastructure, facilities, transportation systems, and even emergency services. For our next act, we'll combine everything we've learned about attractions with larger, park-wide concepts to create a complete experience.

Until then I'm going 10-7.

Chapter 45: Welcome to My Theme Park

During the first part of this book we had some fun looking at all the creative disciplines involved in theme park design. As the chapters progressed, we focused more and more on the technical aspects of theme Park engineering, delving in great detail into the fields of Show Control, Ride Control, and Audio / Video Engineering.

Now we're going to put it all together. We'll start by looking at the history of theme parks, beginning with the granddaddy of them all, Disneyland. (There are those who would claim the first theme park was Tivoli Gardens, but I argue that it began as an amusement park and is still evolving into a theme park.)

Next we'll look at why building a theme park is a lot like building a city—only more so.

Then we'll sweat the details—all those real world issues about site planning, infrastructure and services that our guests want to know nothing about.

And finally I'll bring things full circle and finish that theme park design I started way back at the beginning.

It's time to play the role of billionaire eccentric, and create an entire theme park, just the way it suits us. Will you be Bill Gates or Michael Jackson? Walt Disney or Steven Spielberg?

What will your theme park be like? Will it be educational, exciting, emotionally involving, tasty, fun?

It's up to you. As they say in the trade, "The money cannons are loaded."

So come on, light the fuse. It'll be fun.

Chapter 46: Why Disneyland Will Fail

There were amusement parks before Disneyland, but most people agree there were no theme parks. Looking back, the concept of the theme park seems an obvious one, guaranteed for success. But that was far from the case. In the 1950s it was easy to find reasons why Disneyland might fail

At the 1997 International Association of Amusement Parks and Attractions (IAAPA) trade show in Orlando Florida, industry guru Bob Rogers of BRC Imagination Arts discussed the beginnings of Disneyland. In his speech he described how Walt Disney's ideas about theme parks were considered foolish whimsy by the rest of the amusement industry:

Theme park lore has it that Walt Disney conceived Disneyland during a visit to a Los Angeles amusement park, while watching his daughters ride a merry-go-round. But the real story starts on a stormy November night in a hotel room in Chicago.

It is 1953. Seven men sit in a smoke filled room, drinking Chivas Regal and puffing on Cuban cigars.

Walt Disney is not there. The three men representing him know little about theme parks. The other four men are giants of the amusement park industry. They represent parks from all around the country: Chicago, New Orleans, San Francisco, and even Coney Island. They are there to tell the others why Walt's ideas will fail.

- Disneyland will fail because it lacks the proven moneymakers. There is no roller coaster, no Ferris wheel, no Tunnel of Love, no hotdogs carts, and no beer. Worst of all, there are no redemption games. There are no midway barkers, and no midway. After paying at the front ticket booth, customers can keep their wallets in their pockets.
- Disneyland will fail because custom rides will never work. They cost too much to design, they will break too often,

and the ride capacity will be too low. Only off-the-shelf rides are cheap enough to operate economically. And the public doesn't know the difference.

- Disneyland will fail because a lot of the stuff in the park produces no revenue. Castles and pirate ships are cute, but there's no economic reason for them.
- Disneyland will fail because you can't operate an amusement park year-round. 120 days per year is the best you can do.
- Disneyland will fail because it has only one entrance. You need entrances on all sides for closer parking and easier access.
- Disneyland will fail because all those design details and fancy finishes cost too much. The same applies to elaborate landscaping and fastidious cleanliness. The guests will destroy the place no matter what you do, so you might as well do it cheaply.
- Disneyland will fail because the average customer spends only about 1 dollar per capita in an amusement park.

Two years later Disneyland opened. Per capita spending was $4.50. By the second year it was $6.00.

How did Walt do it?

Before Disneyland the average guest stayed at an amusement park less than two hours. But Disneyland's pleasant and interesting ambience invited guests to stay longer—an unprecedented seven hours. Because guests were there longer, they spent more on food, souvenirs and rides.

Walt created this ambience by focusing not just on the attractions, but also on the space between the attractions. He viewed the park from the guest's perspective. He never let his guests forget that they were someplace special. And that made them special.

Most importantly, before Disneyland attractions were designed by engineers, architects, operators or curators.

Disneyland was designed by storytellers.

That is why it forced those industry experts to eat their words.

Building Walt's Dream

Walt's original idea was for a "magical little park" where kids and their parents could have fun together. This sounds pretty mundane today, but at the time it was revolutionary.

His original plan was to develop the eight acres adjacent to his Burbank Studios, but he soon realized that would not be enough land for his expanding vision.

It was also clear it would take a lot of money.

"I could never convince the financiers that Disneyland was feasible," Walt said, "because dreams offer too little collateral."

Walt hit upon the idea to use television to both finance and publicize his new park. The show, on ABC-TV, would document the park's progress from drawing board to opening day. It was called "Disneyland".

Walt and his brother Roy began by purchasing 160 acres of orange groves and walnut trees near the Santa Ana Freeway and Harbor Boulevard in Anaheim, California.

That was the easy part. Then came the questions.

How do you build a castle in an orange grove? Create a river? Make animals move?

For answers, Walt turned to his movie studio, and eventually created a design company, WED Enterprises, named after his initials—Walter Elias Disney. (In the 1980's the company was renamed Walt Disney Imagineering.)

The park was conceived around five lands:

Main Street, USA would recreate the turn-of-the-century town. "For those of us who remember the carefree time it recreates, Main Street will bring back happy memories," Walt said. "For younger visitors, it is an adventure in turning back the calendar to the days of grandfather's youth." At the end of Main Street, Walt placed Sleeping Beauty's castle, a "weenie," as he called it. He said, "What you need is a weenie, which says to people come this way.' People won't go down a long corridor unless there's something promising at the end. You have to have something that beckons them to walk this way.'"

Adventureland would be an exotic and far away place. "To create a land that would make this dream reality, we pictured ourselves far from civilization, in the remote jungles of Asia and Africa," Walt said.

Frontierland would take us to the pioneer days of the American frontier. "All of us have cause to be proud of our country's history, shaped by the pioneering spirit of our forefathers," Walt said, "Our adventures are designed to give you the feeling of having lived, even for a short while, during our country's pioneer days."

Fantasyland would be a place where dreams could come true. "What youngster has not dreamed of flying with Peter Pan over moonlit London, or tumbling into Alice's nonsensical Wonderland?" Walt said. "In Fantasyland, these classic stories of everyone's youth have become realities for youngsters—of all ages—to participate in."

And Tomorrowland would provide a peek into the future. "Tomorrow can be a wonderful age," Walt said. "Our scientists today are opening the doors of the Space Age to achievements that will benefit our children and generations to come. The Tomorrowland attractions have been designed to give you an opportunity to participate in adventures that are a living blueprint of our future." Even Walt realized, of course, that Tomorrowland would be "obsolete the day it opens." But he also said "Disneyland will never be finished."

Of course, imagining a theme park is easier than building one. Construction began July 21st, 1954.

Things did not go as planned, right from the start.

To begin clearing the land, orange trees were marked with red and green paper, to indicate which were to be saved and which to be bulldozed. Unfortunately, no one noticed that the bulldozer operator was colorblind until all the trees were gone.

When it came time to fill the Rivers of America—the waterway that surrounds Tom Sawyer's Island—everyone was excited to see the valve opened and water begin to flow into the channel. But as fast as it poured forth, it sank into the sandy soil and disappeared. Weeks of experimentation and hundreds of loads of clay were required to fix the problem.

It was undoubtedly an interesting time to live near the Santa Ana Freeway. The alert observer might see a steam locomotive pass, or perhaps an entire deck of a paddlewheeler. Toward the end, trees, ride vehicles, carousel horses castle turrets, keel boats, mules, horse cars, a rocket ship, and plastic jungle animals formed an endless cavalcade.

The park opened only 12 months after the start of construction. The final cost of $17 million seems ludicrously small by today's standards, but in 1955 it represented a tremendous leap of faith.

Opening day was unforgettable. But it, too, did not go as planned.

6000 invitations had been mailed for the televised event. But by mid-afternoon over 28,000 ticket holders arrived. Most of the tickets were counterfeit.

A 15-day heat wave had elevated temperatures to 110 degrees Fahrenheit. Asphalt, poured only the night before, was still steaming. In the heat of the day, the ladies' high heeled shoes became mired in it.

A plumbers' strike had prevented the installation of most of the park's water fountains, leaving the guests to sweat it out, and complain it was a ploy to sell more sodas.

But standing in Town Square for the opening ceremony, Walt could look out across the crowd and see the fulfillment of his dream: a truly Magic Kingdom. In true show business tradition, Art Linkletter, Bob Cummings and Ronald Reagan(!) provided live TV coverage of the whole event—glitches and all.

The main dedication plaque of Disneyland still stands at the bottom of the flagpole in Town Square. The plaque shows Walt took his park seriously as a work of culture and as a positive celebration of shared values. Before Disneyland, mere amusement parks didn't take themselves seriously. If anything, they celebrated the darker side of our nature. Walt's seriousness—and optimism—underscore how strikingly different Disneyland was from its predecessors:

"To all who come to this happy place: welcome. Disneyland is your land. Here age relives fond memories of the past... and here youth may savor the challenge and promise of the future. Disneyland is dedicated to the ideals, the dreams and the hard facts that have created America... with the hope that it will be a source of joy and inspiration to all the world. -- Walt Disney"

Despite its rocky opening and slow initial attendance, word-of-mouth soon spread, and Disneyland was a success. By 1965, 10 years after opening, Disneyland had entertained 50 million guests.

Today, the combined Disney parks host that many visitors each year.

Chapter 47: Building a City

Let's take a trip to Reedy Creek.

The Reedy Creek Improvement District is similar to a county. It's comprised of 25,000 acres, about twice the size of Manhattan. There are two cities in Reedy Creek: Bay Lake and Lake Buena Vista. As with any city or county, the Reedy Creek Improvement District derives its income from taxes and fees collected within its boundaries. It is governed by a Board of Supervisors, with an election every two years.

Reedy Creek is not a small place. On an average day its population (although transitory) places it somewhere in the middle of the list of the 100 largest urban areas in the United States. On a busy summer day its population rivals that of Pittsburgh.

As with any populous area, Reedy Creek provides extensive services. It operates its own landfill, sewage treatment plant, and recycling center. Its road maintenance department is responsible for over 100 lane miles of roadways. It operates three fire stations and six ambulances with trained paramedics. The district is responsible for 47 miles of canals.

Reedy Creek is far ahead of the country in many ways. Its building codes, emergency services, and environmental policies are extremely progressive.

Reedy Creek's building and safety codes are some of the most stringent in the United States, and are referenced by cities nationwide. Nearly every structure is equipped with fire sprinklers, including nearly 300 acres of support buildings.

Almost one-third of the Reedy Creek Improvement District is set aside as a wildlife conservation area. It is home to one of the nation's largest concentrations of bald eagles, as well as other protected species including sandhill cranes, wood storks, and crested caracaras.

Reedy Creek's wastewater treatment plant processes 10 million gallons of water per day, reclaiming much of it for irrigation.

The Material Recovery Facility processes 45 tons of recyclables every day, including paper, plastic, glass, steel, aluminum, and cardboard. Amazingly, this represents about 56 percent of all the waste in the district. That is double the rate of most other counties. In the past ten years more than one billion pounds of material has been recycled.

Each month nearly 40,000 pounds of leftover food is donated to the Second Harvest Food Bank, which serves the hungry. About 3000 tons of food waste is used as livestock feed each year.

Sewage byproducts, landscape waste, paper, degradable construction debris and ground wooden pallets are combined to produce 50,000 pounds of compost each day, some of it used as a soil additive along the roadways.

All printed materials and corrugated shipping containers purchased in the district are made from 100 percent recycled and recyclable materials.

Over 20,000,000,000 kilowatt hours (kWh) of energy are consumed within the district each year. By comparison, your household monthly energy consumption is probably a couple thousand kWh. By installing energy-efficient lighting throughout the district, Reedy Creek has saved nearly 100,000,000 kWh per year.

A few final statistics may shed some light on where the Reedy Creek improvement District is located. In Reedy Creek they:

- Wash 52 million pounds of laundry per year.
- Dry-clean 32,000 costumes per day.
- Cook 7,000,000 hamburgers per year.
- Pop 265,000 pounds of popcorn per year.
- Pour 46 million Cokes each year.
- Offer 6000 different foods every day
- Sell enough mouse ear hats every year for each resident of Pittsburgh.

The boundaries of the Reedy Creek Improvement District align, approximately, with those of Walt Disney World. In essence, Reedy Creek is Disney. It was created in 1967 by the Florida Legislature as a special taxing district—similar to a county—so that Disney could manage its own affairs.

As you can see, constructing a theme park truly is like building a city.

But cities grow like topsy. Most theme parks are planned out in advance. True, some suffer through growing pains. Disneyland has been trying to squeeze more attractions into their tiny plot of land for more than three decades. And they forgot to aim the Disney MGM Studios entrance toward the parking lot... or to allow for any expansion.

But these days most theme parks are master-planned far in advance. More than 20 years after opening, Epcot still has plenty of plots left for more World Showcase pavilions. And when they began construction of the Magic Kingdom in the late 1960s they built a maze of soon to be underground utility corridors on top of the ground, then covered them with dirt scooped from the swamp, thus creating a network of concealed access tunnels and a lake, all in one operation.

Cities rarely benefit from that much planning. That's why the streets aren't straight, the utilities aren't buried, and there's an ugly self-serve gas station next to the Fine Arts Museum.

Chapter 48: Sweating the Details

Creating a great theme park doesn't mean just inventing some wonderful attractions. It takes the site work and infrastructure of a city to make a theme park work.

No theme park is complete without the people who make it run, and some of those people haven't been mentioned before. They provide vital services to your guests. Some of those services even represent profit centers.

Was that the sound of cash registers I just heard?

Site Work

The first step in building any theme park is the site work. This begins with clearing the land, and then continues through all manner of terraforming. At Walt Disney World this meant draining a swamp and the construction of 47 miles of canal.

While it may no longer be politically correct to drain a swamp, huge amounts of dirt still need to be moved around to construct most theme parks. Theme parks with elevation changes are visually more interesting than flat theme parks; so most designers take advantage of any natural topography to create an interesting landscape. A great example of using the natural topography is at Legoland California, where the natural hillsides above the Pacific Ocean form an interesting variety of hills and lakes, making a perfect theme park setting.

Even when the land is completely flat extensive earthmoving is sometimes needed. In Florida the porous, sandy soil won't support the weight of theme park-sized buildings. Prior to the start of construction the ground must be "pre-charged" to compact the soil and drive out groundwater. You can see this taking place wherever huge mounds of dirt are piled at the future site of buildings.

Sometimes the earth isn't so much "moved" as it is "delivered". Tokyo Disneyland and Tokyo Disney Seas are constructed on fill dumped into Tokyo Bay. Before 1980, the site of Cinderella's Castle would have been better suited to fishing.

Not that you'd want to eat any fish that came from Tokyo Bay.

Transportation

Even before earthmoving begins, thought must be given to how a theme park's transportation systems will work. In the United States, most theme park visitors arrive by car. This means massive parking lots must be near the theme park entrance, or near transportation systems that lead to the theme park entrance.

At Walt Disney World, Walt didn't want the reality of the everyday world of parking lots and fast food restaurants to impinge upon the Magic Kingdom, the way they had at the original Disneyland. So he purchased 25,000 acres in Central Florida. This was enough land to relegate the fast food restaurants to the distant fringes of the property (although lately a few McDonald's have found their way into guest areas).

He also located the main parking lot for the Magic Kingdom on the other side of the Seven Seas Lagoon. Guests arrive at the Magic Kingdom by either paddlewheeler or monorail, so their themed experience begins even before they enter Main Street.

Visitors to theme parks outside the United States are more likely to arrive by mass transportation. While there is still a massive parking lot at Paris Disneyland, the train station was constructed right outside the entrance, providing easy access from anywhere in Europe.

Transportation between attractions is important to. Walt Disney first recognized this need with the horse drawn carriages on Main Street. On a larger scale, double-decker buses and ferryboats transport guests around Epcot's World Showcase.

Even when parks are intended primarily for pedestrian traffic, they must still be constructed so that during the night maintenance personnel can maneuver trucks, cherry pickers and other service vehicles within the park.

Most parks also have a periphery road that runs around the outside of the attractions, providing discrete daytime access for vehicles and workers.

Power

There is one thing that theme parks need more of than anything else and I'm not talking about guests.

Theme parks use a lot of power. In the case of Walt Disney World, 20 billion kWh each year.

That's a big number, but to most of us it's just a statistic. Let's think about it a minute.

Say that light by your bed consumes 50 watts. Twenty of them would be one kilowatt. Leave them all on for one hour, and you've used one-kilowatt hour. After a day, that's 24 kWh.

So in a little over 2000 years you'd have equaled Walt Disney World's annual power bill.

Now if only we could find light bulbs that would last that long.

All that power needs to be delivered somehow. We've gone through most of this book without having to resort to a formula. But just for fun, let's look at one simple equation. Besides, you can use it to impress your friends or entertain people at a party. Or not.

$P = IV$

There. That wasn't so bad.

It means: Power is equal to Current times Voltage.

To understand electricity, it's easiest to think of it like water.

Current is a measure of the flow of electricity. See, it is like water.

More water will flow through a hose than through a drinking straw. And more still will flow through a storm drain. So it's sort of like the cross-section of the pipe. But keep in mind that drinking straws are cheaper than storm drains.

Voltage is like pressure. Poke a hole in the side of a drinking glass and the water will dribble out. Poke a hole in the bottom of a 50,000 gallon storage tank, and the water will shoot out in a long stream.

If the hole in the drinking glass is large, the stream will be wide. That's low voltage but high current.

If the hole in the storage tank is a pinhole, the stream will be narrow. That's high voltage but low current.

Either way, it might take the same amount of time to fill a bucket. The bucket of water is the delivered power. And power is what we need a fixed amount of.

So we can supply power to our theme park using either high voltage and really skinny wire, or low voltage and really thick wire. Obviously, skinny wire is cheaper.

That's why power is distributed cross-country using those high-tension towers. The voltage is typically 13,800 volts, but the wire is relatively skinny.

Unfortunately, plugging your vacuum cleaner into 13,800 volts will not get the job done one hundred times as fast. And sticking your finger into a light socket with that voltage will not only cancel your ticket, it might vaporize the evidence.

So these high transmission voltages must be transformed to lower voltages for use in the parks. Our theme park attractions may use voltages as high as 440 volts for motors, but mostly they're going to need the same kind of power we use at home.

This is accomplished with giant transformers. One set of transformers in an electrical substation at the edge of our theme park property drops the voltage to some intermediate level. Smaller transformers near the attractions drop it to working levels.

Because our theme park is so dependent upon power we must design this distribution system with care. In June 2002 a small fire in an electrical substation closed Epcot. It was the first time in Walt Disney World history that an individual park had been forced to close. (The only other WDW park closures since the Magic Kingdom's opening in 1971 were caused by concern about Hurricane Floyd and September 11th. That's an amazing record of operational readiness.)

We also need to hide all that ugly power stuff from our guests. Remember, they came to escape from the real world. They don't want to be reminded that they left the bedside lamp on.

Air Conditioning

One of the major consumers of all that power is air conditioning. People typically go to theme parks during the summer, when the weather is hot. A room full of hot, sweaty people isn't a pleasant environment. So theme parks work hard to cool them off.

In large theaters this is done by blowing cool air up underneath the seats and removing hot air near the ceiling. This carries the smells of all those hot, sweaty bodies up away from the audience.

When you consider the typical theme park has hundreds of thousands of square feet of air-conditioned space, it's easy to see that efficiency is vital.

At large theme parks the most efficient way to air condition is by distributing chilled water from a central refrigeration plant to the individual attractions. The theory is that one gigantic heat exchanger is more efficient than many distributed ones, just as central air-conditioning in your home is more efficient than dozens of window air conditioners.

Of course, there are a few places that don't need air conditioning. We did a visitor center inside the arctic circle once. And there's always the splash zone—the first 14 rows of seats in Shamu Stadium. That ice cold water will cool you right off.

Bathrooms, Sewer & Water

Theme parks use a lot of water. During a typical day Walt Disney World reclaims 10 million gallons of the stuff, reusing it for irrigation or returning it to Florida's aquifer.

A lot of this water goes into bathrooms, so the efficiency of plumbing fixtures plays a major role in water conservation.

One of the more unusual jobs of my career was programming Epcot's Park Function Controller. This computer at Epcot Central was responsible for many park wide functions, including turning on the exterior lighting a different times each day depending upon when the sun set. Another role of the Park Function Controller was to control the automatic flushing of the urinals in the men's rooms.

Try putting that on your resume.

Communications

When someone says "communications", most of us think about telephones. But theme parks have many different ways of distributing information.

Even in 1982 Epcot used fiber optics to transmit some data between Epcot Central and the various pavilions. In addition, the cable vault contained thousands of miles of copper wiring.

These days not just telephone but also computer data in many forms must be distributed everywhere within the park. Even cash registers are electronically connected to credit processing centers. The communications system is also integrated with security and monitoring systems such as fire alarms and closed-circuit television.

A wise theme park designer will allow for new communications lines to be pulled through unused conduit, because it's a safe bet that the communications of the future will require interconnections that don't even exist today.

More Site Work—Landscaping

Our infrastructure—water lines, sewer lines, electricity, and communications conduit—are all in the ground. Now we can start pouring some concrete and building attractions

fade to calendar pages tearing away and fluttering off in the breeze

Whew. That was fast. Those attractions look really great. But, ummm..., there's a problem.

This theme park looks like the Mojave Desert. Or worse. I don't think your guests are going to want to visit a place that has all the charm of a federal penitentiary.

That's why theme parks spend millions of dollars on landscaping. Disney World alone has about 4000 acres of landscaping.

In some parks the value of the landscaping exceeds that of the attractions. It's the finishing touch that creates a welcoming, relaxing environment for guests.

The selection of landscaping depends upon the theming of the park, and the local climate. It was a real challenge building a jungle boat cruise in Tokyo Disneyland. The vegetation had to look tropical, yet withstand Tokyo's surprisingly frigid winters. Ever seen a hippo with snow on its back?

Security

In a perfect world, guests would arrive after opening time, behave in an orderly fashion all day, and depart before dark.

Heh, heh.

In the real world they try to sneak in, drink too many beers, and hide in the bushes after closing time.

Sometimes nature takes care of this problem. There was the guy who hid in the bushes next to Shamu Stadium at SeaWorld until the park closed, then went for a swim with the killer whales. No, they didn't eat him. He died of hypothermia in the chilled water.

But for problems that nature doesn't take care of, there's the security staff. They control access to the non-guest areas of the park, handle disturbances, prevent shoplifting, and make sure the park is clear of guests after closing. In times of heightened security concerns —and on grad nights—they also check for weapons and contraband. They're kept busy in other ways as well on grad nights, but we won't go there

These day, for liability reasons, having a dedicated theme park security team and an integrated surveillance system is a must.

Fire Control

There are three fire stations at Walt Disney World. Located near each of the major parks, they can respond quickly to emergencies.

Structure fires are rare, since all of the buildings have sprinkler systems. But there are also traffic accidents, and in the evening the occasional wildfire started by wayward fireworks.

Smaller theme parks may not have an official fire department, but they all have fire response procedures.

Emergency Medical

Walt Disney World also maintains a fleet of six ambulances, but, surprisingly, no hospital. There is a hospital not far from the property, though, and injured or sick guests can be transported rapidly.

Equally important are the first aid stations located throughout the parks. On a busy day a single theme park entertains more than 50,000 people. With that many visitors, injuries and illness are inevitable. So the wise park designer tries to provide guests with easy access to health care professionals.

On March 31st, 2002, the Wood-Mirlo family visited Disneyland. They were celebrating their son Dallas' eighth birthday. Mother Wendy was pregnant, but heck, the baby wasn't due until May 1st. So off they headed down Main Street.

Then Wendy's water broke.

The park staff came to life. Disney nurses raced to the scene, along with paramedics and the Disney police. They rushed Wendy into a security room and gathered around her.

"It's OK, mom," said Dallas, trying to comfort his upset mother.

Her husband held her head in his lap.

"I need to push," Wendy said.

The paramedic told her to hold on; he wanted to get her to a hospital.

It didn't work out that way.

Austin Ray Mirlo, 7 lbs. 5-1/4 ounces, was born at 11:30 AM.

"It's a boy!" the paramedic cried out. The crowd of Disneyland nurses, paramedics and police broke into applause.

The park invited Dallas to select two birthday gifts from a nearby shop, and the family was given return tickets for another day.

Austin was the third baby born at Disneyland.

Food Services

It takes a lot of people to produce 7 million inedible hamburgers a year. The logistics of staffing, stocking and maintaining a theme park's food service is equivalent to operating dozens—or even hundreds—of restaurants.

The best food service is themed to the park itself. Much of World Showcase's raison d'etre—Tish, that's French!—is the variety of international cuisines served in its restaurants. Disney's Animal Kingdom offers a number of African themed dining experiences, and the Animal Kingdom Lodge serves authentic African cuisine and wines.

One has to be careful with this, sometimes. You won't find dolphin on the menu at SeaWorld.

Kitchens

Why are kitchens listed here separate from restaurants?

Because in theme parks there isn't a one-to-one correspondence. Much of the food is prepared in central kitchens and delivered to the food service locations. Even sit down restaurants might be cleverly located so they open onto different areas of the park, yet share a single kitchen. Disneyland's Plaza Pavilion on Main Street and the Tiki restaurant in Adventureland are really the same building.

The rationale for this is that kitchens are expensive. They have special facilities requirements that must be accommodated during construction. Not only are they major consumers of electricity, water and sewer, they also have to dispose of toxic waste: cooking grease.

Most restaurants have a grease handling system that routes grease to an underground tank outside, were it can be pumped out and disposed of appropriately. You don't want this job.

Merchandising

Let's not forget the final way that Disneyland upped per capita spending. Selling stuff.

Mouse ear hats and Tinker Bell wands cost next to nothing to make, and sell like hotcakes in a theme park environment.

Of course, not all theme park souvenirs are merely "stuff". At Universal Studios Florida and Disney MGM Studios you can buy authentic Hollywood memorabilia. And Epcot's World Showcase sells fine crystal and porcelain from around the world.

Accommodations

Here's the ultimate way to boost your theme park revenues: build hotels!

Be careful you don't build too few, like they did in the early days of Walt Disney World, when only the Contemporary and Polynesian resorts existed, and hundreds of low-end motels opened up in nearby Kissimmee.

But don't build too many, either, like they did at Paris Disneyland, where several had to be mothballed until attendance grew.

Disney pioneered the idea of continuing a park's theming right into the hotel when they partnered with the Disneyland Hotel, connecting it to the monorail ride. Fast-forward 35 years—The Animal Kingdom Lodge lets guests look out upon an African savannah filled with wildlife.

Chapter 49: Steve Alcorn's Time Portal and Floating Lily Pad World

Remember my attraction ideas from early in this book? There was a magic time portal that took you from a library into a medieval village where a fair was in full swing. And I had those floating antigravity lily pads, too.

Well now I'm going to put it all together and create—tadaa!— Steve Alcorn's Time Portal And Floating Lily Pad World.

Has a ring to it, doesn't it?

Well, OK, so the idea needs work. At least it's a start.

Maybe the attractions in my theme park should be more closely themed

Hey, I've got an idea. What if the whole park is about time travel? Forget this lily pad stuff. I was having trouble with the antigravity part, anyway. Let's create a succession of attractions that are all accessed through a time portal from the library.

Hmmm. Let's think about this.

We plunge the library into darkness, flood it with fog, snatch away the walls, and voila! Our guests are in a different time. We could make it a surprise, so they'd never know what time they'd end up in, sort of like that old Time Tunnel television show.

Nahhh. That became annoying after a few episodes. And our guests would get annoyed, too. They need to be able to select what time they'd like to visit.

Maybe we should have a separate library for each attraction. That would make the transformation effect easier.

But it would be hard to explain to the guests.

Hmmm

How about if it seems to the guests that they're always going into the same library, but it's really different libraries depending upon where they want to go?

No, that doesn't make any sense. Why would one building have so many different libraries?

Could it be a house, where each different room took you to a different spot? Let's see, the kitchen could take you to ancient Rome, the living room could take you to the Ming Dynasty, and the bathroom could take you to New Jersey no, this isn't working.

How about a time travel research facility? It could have a long hallway with doors opening off of it into separate laboratories. Each laboratory could transport you to a different era. That era would be the subject of research for that particular laboratory. Before the transformation, the lab benches and shelves could contain research materials and curios associated with that time period.

I like it.

It's simple, easy to convey the story line to guests, and has almost unlimited potential. In addition to my medieval fair, I'll have dinosaurs, ancient Egypt, Rome, Victorian London, the Wild West, and maybe a futuristic Los Angeles, sort of like Blade Runner. I'll have to be careful with that last one. Futuristic attractions always end up looking dated. So mine will intentionally be weird, or retro looking.

That's a good, solid start to a new theme park concept. (If anyone wealthy out there would like to bankroll the idea, you can have it for free. I'd just like a lifetime pass, please. Oh and you know where to buy your show control equipment, right?)

So why have I gone through this thought process on paper?

To remind you that Story is King.

And if story was important in an individual attraction, it's even more important for an entire park. Collections of attractions that don't convey a simple, compelling story end up disjointed and confusing.

***

So that's what it takes to construct an entire theme park.We've looked at the infrastructure needs of our park, and the services we'll need to provide, and have peeked at some successful examples.

Constructing a theme park truly is a lot like building a city.

As we wind things up we'll gaze into our crystal ball and make some predictions about the future of themed entertainment. We'll also take a look at how the business of themed entertainment might fit into your future.

Hey, how's that for a weenie?

Chapter 50: Other Markets

Our ride on the Theme Park Design roller coaster is approaching the unload station. Like any good themed attraction, it's been exciting, interesting, and educational. Heck, we even got to spend a billion bucks! But like any good themed attraction, it ends too soon.

Before the vehicle comes to a stop, though, let's get out our binoculars, our microscope, and our crystal ball, and take a good look around.

With our binoculars we'll survey the wide world of themed entertainment, and find out what other markets there are besides theme parks.

With our microscope we'll take a closer look ourselves, and see where we might fit into the themed entertainment job sector. More importantly, we'll discuss some strategies for getting that job.

And finally, with our crystal ball, we'll gaze into the future of themed entertainment to see where it's headed, and maybe even make a few wishes.

Now hang on; this last stretch of track has a lot of twists and turns.

Bigger and Better

Building theme parks is kind of like eating potato chips. Once you've had one, you're almost compelled to move on to the next. Just ask Disney.

With four parks in Florida, two in California, two in France, two in Japan, one in China and more on the way, Disney's clearly placing a bet on the continued financial viability of large parks. And the news is encouraging. Parks on which they spent a lot of money—like Tokyo Disney Seas—are extremely popular. The investment is paying off with high attendance and a high rate of returning guests. Other parks, where the budgets were skimpy and the theming was thin, are not faring as well.

Universal Studios has had mixed results with its parks. After a rocky opening, Universal Studios Florida now has respectable attendance figures. And their Islands of Adventure is widely regarded as one of the world's best theme parks. But after a very successful opening, Universal Studios Japan has had trouble attracting return guests, and the formula is still being tweaked.

And then there are rehabs. In the words of Walt Disney, "Disneyland will never be completed. It will continue to grow as long as there is imagination left in the world." That attitude prevails, and ensures that all of the Disney parks will constantly be changing and evolving. It's sometimes painful for those of us in the industry. We work on a project countless hours, toiling until that fabled 2am on opening day, then watch our creation being demolished a decade later. But that constant flux guarantees the parks will remain fresh and vibrant. And we'll remain employed.

It's unlikely that another park like Epcot will ever be built. Nearly every system, every technology, and every venue was new and revolutionary. Future parks will use more purchased rides, and more guaranteed formulas. But that doesn't mean they need to be boring. Legoland makes up for conservative ride technologies with terrific theming and a precisely targeted appeal: 3 to 12-year-olds and their parents. Six Flags pushes the ride envelope, concentrating on the fastest and most exciting hard iron rides, with minimal theming. The SeaWorld parks and Busch Gardens Tampa focus on animals, and invite guest interaction. Any of these approaches can be successful, if carefully designed to ensure a quality experience for each guest.

With many other brands also solidly committed to worldwide expansion of their theme parks, the future is likely to hold more and better parks for all of us.

Smaller and Closer

Not every park needs to be a giant. Tivoli Gardens has demonstrated this principle for over a hundred years. Smaller regional parks can be successful, even if they are seasonal. Busch Gardens Williamsburg and King's Dominion are examples of successful regional parks. Had it not been canceled due to local opposition, Disney's America would've been another. Except for Disney's parks, European theme parks are all regional. Europa Park in Germany, Liseberg in Sweden, and the UK's Alton Towers are all very popular.

Another type of smaller attraction is the public venue. In Las Vegas alone you can wander beneath a four block long video screen, watch a fountain show or volcanic eruption, and experience a pirate ship battle—including a sinking ship—all for free, from the public sidewalks.

There is still a market for smaller scale, local experiences, and we'll see more of these in the future.

Vertical Markets

Some parks cater to only one specific market segment. Legoland is really just for kids and their parents. Some of the hard iron parks appeal almost exclusively to teenagers.

I believe it's possible to design parks for even narrower vertical markets, provided that the return on investment is properly analyzed. A Native American experience located on Indian land near a major highway in the American West is an obvious example of an untapped market. NASA's Space Center Houston and Kennedy Space Center are both major visitor centers. Is there room for expansion into a full-scale theme park?

The ultimate vertical markets are corporate ones. Visitor centers, such as the one at Coca Cola's Atlanta headquarters combine the best elements of themed entertainment with a pitch to buy more product.

Trade shows are also making more and more use of themed entertainment techniques. Automobile shows, in particular, use high budget, state of the art audio, video and lighting to generate excitement about the manufacturers' latest offerings.

LBE's

Location Based Entertainment (LBE) is any form of entertainment tied to a particular location other than your home. LBE includes amusement parks, theme parks, ride films, large-scale arcades, bowling alleys, pool halls, water parks, casinos, and multiplex movie theaters. I suppose sporting events should also be included in the list, but no one does.

Obviously, LBE has been around for more than a century. But in the 1990s there was a real explosion of LBE startups, focusing on high-end multiplayer interactive and virtual reality computer games. This form of LBE was thought to be the next big thing. Then came the shakeout, and few of those new ventures exist today.

What went wrong?

Many of the new startups were based upon virtual reality or elaborate multiplayer computer simulations. The cost of development for some of these installations exceeded $1000 per square foot, and yet the constrained indoor space in which they operated provided limited revenue generating potential. In short, the bottom line added up to a negative number.

A lot of these facilities didn't properly analyze their capacity. Restricted entryways, slow throughput, and a high spectator to player ratio resulted in many missed revenue forecasts.

Also, most LBE's failed to carry a story line; there was no theming. A roomful of noisy simulators is only appealing to a narrow market segment, and only for limited time. And many LBE's failed to distinguish themselves from one another. One roomful of noisy simulators is a lot like the next. Without clear branding, LBE's failed to attract a repeat audience.

Few LBE's were located in areas with high enough traffic to support their required attendance. Many were in shopping malls. But malls are sparsely populated most weekdays. Teenagers aren't available during school hours to feed dollars into those expensive simulators. Most LBE's generated 80 percent of their income during the 20 percent of the week between Friday afternoon and Sunday morning. Some LBE's located in prime tourist areas fared better.

As home computers became more powerful, much of the LBE experience was available in your family room. Spectacular graphics and accurate real-time simulation were once the exclusive domain of the powerful, expensive computer systems installed in LBE's. Now the most modest desktop computer exceeds their performance.

The interaction between different players was also a unique selling feature of LBE's. But in the world of Internet connectivity, multi-user games involving thousands of people are now commonplace.

But the LBE situation isn't hopeless. One needs to look no further than video games to find an example of an entertainment technology that rose from the ashes.

Video games arrived in force in the early 1980s. Atari, Nintendo, Sega, and a dozen other took off like a rocket, and that first Christmas stores couldn't keep the cartridges on the shelves. But by the late 1980s there was a tremendous shakeout. Public interest waned. But new technologies, PC-based games, and exciting new graphics and storylines revive the industry. Sony's PlayStation and Microsoft's X-box upped the ante. Video games are thriving. It might be possible to orchestrate a similar comeback for LBE's.

To survive, LBE's need to offer a social environment that's not available to someone sitting in his or her family room. A truly successful LBE must involve all of its players in the game. The content is what matters. There needs to be a gathering place where people can meet—perhaps a pre-briefing room—and a cafe, bar or restaurant where they can dawdle afterwards, to talk about their shared experience. You may be able to join thousands of people online from the computer in your family room, but you can't chat with them about the game over drinks afterwards.

The future of LBE's is unclear. It will take good theming, and a better understanding of the customer before LBE's become a major force in themed entertainment.

FEC's

The Family Entertainment Center (FEC) is a type of LBE that doesn't depend upon sophisticated networked computers. This market segment also blossomed in the 1990s, and then experienced a shakeout.

Discovery Zone was the leading FEC. As with most FEC's, the focus of Discovery Zone was on "soft play"—indoor obstacle courses that kids explore, climb through, and slide down.

Discovery Zone was wise to include quiet areas for adults to hang out while their kids played, and a cafe to encourage guests to stay longer. They also provided party rooms for birthdays, and a small arcade for additional revenue.

But the concept wasn't successful because of that old 80/20 problem. 80 percent of revenues were generated during 20 percent of the week between Friday afternoon and Sunday morning. There just weren't enough birthday parties to pay the bills.

Today only the largest and best located FEC's still exist. The FEC is still a concept that bears watching. People are willing to spend a lot of money on their kids, and the right mix of story, environment, and revenue model might still lead to a successful concept.

Theming the World

Theming doesn't stop with LBE's and FEC's. It's trickled down from theme parks to the neighborhood mall, restaurants, and nearly every public space.

But just because a space is themed, doesn't mean it tells a story, or provides an experience. That's still best done in theme parks—and in the occasional smaller facility that transcends its peers. These include some very special visitor centers, museums, and specialty attractions. Such transcendental smaller attractions are my absolute favorite venues, because they're almost always examples of someone doing a lot on a limited budget.

Here's my honor roll of smaller attractions. These are places that go above and beyond in theming, story and guest experience. Their designers should be proud:

- The Star Trek Experience, The Hilton, Las Vegas, NV (defunct)
- Caesar's Magical Empire, Caesar's Palace, Las Vegas, NV (defunct)
- Buccaneer Bay, Treasure Island, Las Vegas, NV (modified)
- Ka, Cirque du Soleil, The MGM Grand, Las Vegas, NV
- NASA's Space Center Houston, Houston, TX
- Nauticus, The National Maritime Center, Norfolk, VA
- The Pro Football Hall of Fame, Canton, OH
- COSI, Columbus, OH
- Madame Tussaud's, Worldwide

How does a theme park designer achieve this kind of excellence? By learning from the successes—and failures—of the past. In the next chapter, one of the industry's legends shares his experience with us.

Chapter 51: Mickey's Ten Commandments

So why do theme parks still fascinate us, in this world where even the neighborhood mall is themed?

It's because of the care with which theme parks are designed, the attention to detail, and the impassioned commitment of theme park designers to transport their guests into an alternate reality.

Every theme park designer should know what's been done in the past. That's why former Walt Disney Imagineering President Marty Sklar developed his ten guidelines for theme park design. They're posted on the wall of his office, and hardly a day goes by that he doesn't look at them.

Here, then, in slightly paraphrased form, is as close as you'll get to the secret of the theme park design universe:

- Know your audience. Don't bore people, talk down to them or lose them by assuming that they know what you know.
- Wear your guest's shoes. Insist that designers, staff and your board members experience your facility as visitors as often as possible.
- Organize the flow of people and ideas. Use good story telling techniques, tell good stories not lectures, lay out your exhibit with a clear logic.
- Create a weenie. Lead visitors from one area to another by creating visual magnets and giving visitors rewards for making the journey.
- Communicate with visual literacy. Make good use of all the non-verbal ways of communication: color, shape, form and texture.
- Avoid overload. Resist the temptation to tell too much, to have too many objects. Don't force people to swallow

more than they can digest. Try to stimulate and provide guidance to those who want more.

- Tell one story at a time. If you have a lot of information, divide it into distinct, logical, organized stories. People can absorb and retain information more clearly if the path to the next concept is clear and logical.
- Avoid contradiction. Clear institutional identity helps give you the competitive edge. The public needs to know who you are and what differentiates you from other institutions they may have seen.
- For every ounce of treatment provide a ton of fun. How do you woo people from all other temptations? Give people plenty of opportunity to enjoy themselves by emphasizing ways that let people participate in the experience and by making your environment rich and appealing to all the senses.
- Keep it up. Never underestimate the importance of cleanliness and routine maintenance. People expect to get a good show every time.

Now that we're expert theme park designers, it would be nice to find an outlet for all these newly acquired talents. In the next chapter we'll look at strategies for finding—and grabbing—the perfect Theme Park Design job.

Chapter 52: How Do I Get That Job?

As I'm sure you can guess, jobs in themed entertainment, and particularly engineering jobs in themed entertainment are extremely rare.

How many of us have said, "When I grow up I want to design attractions for Disney"?

That's exactly what my wife decided, when she was in the third grade. And she grew up to do it. How? By hard work and tenacity, by hitting the right market window, and by being willing to take whatever position was offered.

Walt Disney Imagineering was the only company she applied to, fresh out of college. She did so at a time when Disney was gearing up to build Epcot Center. And she took the menial position of wirelister because she knew it would open doors. It did. Within two years she was responsible for the show control systems throughout a large chunk of Epcot.

But we've been spoiled in this book, getting to eavesdrop on art directors during blue-sky meetings, getting to decide the theming and story of our attraction, and then working through all the technical details ourselves. Even in the smallest theme park design firms no one person gets to do all that. And at a company the size of Walt Disney Imagineering your sphere of influence would be considerably smaller. Maybe just one part of a single system.

The fact is, if you want to do real engineering, your best bet is with one of the smaller theme park design companies. Unfortunately there aren't very many of them. And they do very little hiring.

Let me start by describing my own company.

Alcorn McBride Inc. is one of the only companies in the world that makes products specifically for the themed entertainment industry. We also do some ride systems engineering, but only for particularly sophisticated rides such as Spiderman at Universal Studios Florida.

Our core staff of fifteen people is comprised mostly of degreed electronic engineers with both circuit-level hardware design experience and programming skills.

Our manufacturing, inventory, shipping and repair services are all contracted out, which keeps our overhead extremely low. This allows the engineers to be a real force in product development, from conception through customer support, and all stops in between. They also have input into marketing and sales, write the manuals, design the art for the front panels, and work the trade shows. That's a rare position.

Any job openings we might have are equally rare. We receive dozens of résumés a month from potential candidates. Few of these résumés attract much interest. The reason is not just because of the candidates' qualifications, but also the way the résumés are presented.

I often wonder why someone goes to all the trouble of printing up a nice résumé, and then simply drops it in an envelope and mails it off to some generic company address. Employers handle résumés received this way with the same care they extend to junk mail.

Here's how to get your résumé noticed:

First of all, make sure there's some chance I'll be interested in you. I hire engineers, not manufacturing supervisors, graphic artists, or quality assurance specialists. Sure, I'd like all of my engineers to know something about these fields, but I don't have a large enough company to justify hiring someone with only one of those skills.

We work in themed entertainment, so the second thing I'm going to look for on your résumé is some experience in themed entertainment.

You might argue that this is a chicken and egg scenario, or a Catch-22. How can you develop experience in themed entertainment until you get a job working in themed entertainment?

What I'm interested in is some evidence that you've taken it upon yourself to gain experience in the field, even if it was only a summer job or an unpaid position.

For example, working at a theme park during the summer, volunteering to be part of the technical crew for your local theater group, or even playing in a rock band all indicate a basic interest in entertainment. If your experience is technical, all the better. One of my engineers worked on the lighting crew for the college theater department. He designed a number of microprocessor-controlled gizmos to help do the job.

An excellent way to develop experience in themed entertainment is to volunteer as a technical crew member for one of the many non-commercial haunted houses created every year on Halloween. Some of these are technically complex, and incorporate all of the control systems, audio, and special effects you'd find in a theme park attraction.

The third thing that's vital when sending a résumé is to send it to an individual, not the company as a whole, nor to the Human Resources department. What are the chances of your résumé making it through a 2000-person organization and into the hands of an engineering manager who has a job opening? But if you put his name on the envelope, I guarantee it will.

How do you find out the name of an engineering manager? That usually takes a phone call or two. It seems obvious, but you'd be amazed how few people go to the trouble.

Forth on our list of successful résumé techniques is a personalized letter. It should be brief, but attention getting.

Don't tell me: "I've always wanted to work in Theme Park Design."

Tell me: "Ever since I set my sister's Barbie doll on fire trying to animate it, I've been fascinated by Theme Park Design. And pyrotechnics."

If that opener won't get you a response, nothing will.

Finally, there's the content of your résumé itself. If you're just out of school, your work history is going to be pretty thin. So I'm going to be looking at your outside interests, to see whether they reflect a fascination with theme parks and engineering. I'm also going to read your goal.

Please don't tell me: "I want a challenging position in Theme Park Design." Who doesn't?

I want to know what your goal really is. If you see yourself creating the world's best figure animation system, say it. If you want to travel the world bringing attractions to life, say that. Whatever you're passionate about, your résumé should reflect it.

Having said all that, it's still pretty tough to find an opening in Theme Park Design. Hopefully you'll be looking right before a really big project goes into design. Still, you've got to kiss a lot of frogs before you find that prince. So familiarize yourself with the companies that do what you're interested in.

Nearly every company in the industry belongs to the Themed Entertainment Association (TEA). You can find them online at themeit.com.

Universal, Warner Brothers, Busch, Six Flags and Lego all farm out most of their design work to intermediate companies that do overall theme park design. They in turn farm out the details to other members of the TEA.

A lot of people are interested in designing roller coasters. Historically, just a few companies have made most "hard iron" rides. You'll find the current manufacturers are all members of TEA.

Walt Disney Imagineering does most design work itself. As you might guess, Imagineering gets thousands of résumés, and hires very few. To give you an idea of how few openings there are, despite there being four theme parks at Walt Disney World, my wife is the only WDI show control engineer permanently on staff there.

The best advice I can give you is to keep at it. If you're just starting out, target those summer jobs that will give you a glimpse of the industry from the inside and exploit any and every opportunity to participate in design and installation—even if it's on your own time. Sooner or later your persistence will be rewarded.

Chapter 53: A Wish List

Whenever I walk along the beach I always keep my eyes open, hoping to find a magic lamp washed ashore from some distant land. I like to imagine what I'd wish for if I rubbed the lamp and a genie appeared, and offered me three wishes.

Ruling out the always popular wish for more wishes, and remembering that this is a book about Theme Park Design, here's what I'd wish for our industry:

I wish that the major theme park companies would spend their money better. Far too much of the cost of a major attraction goes into meetings, overhead and managing the process itself, rather than going into the end product. The result is attractions that look cheap, or never quite cross that special line where guests are willing to suspend disbelief. It frustrates me to see $100 million attractions where every penny was obviously pinched in constructing the final product.

When the dollars do get into the end product, the results can be breathtaking. The Spiderman ride at Universal's Islands of Adventure and the Legoland theme park are two examples.

My second wish would be for an end to empty theming. What is all that stuff fastened to the walls in your neighborhood restaurant, anyway? Who decided that we all wanted to eat amidst the overflow of somebody's attic? There's no point to such theming. It's not even really theming; it's just junk.

If a restaurant decorated one room with campaign buttons, another with sporting goods, and a third with classic car memorabilia, and then offered us the choice of which experience we'd like to visit, I'd be the first one to stand and applaud. Or sit down and eat. But I'm tired of the meaningless conglomeration of snow sleds, old gas station signs, and broken tools.

There used to be a terrific restaurant in Orlando with a "Christmas morning" theme. Every table was really a display case filled with toys you haven't seen since you were a little kid. It was great fun. Let's have more of that and less empty theming

My third wish would be for better content. I long for themed experiences that really immerse me in history, or technology, or whatever their specialty may be. Not the shallow experiences of existing theme parks, but a truly involving, consuming, emotionally affecting trip to another world.

We're brought up to think of history as a dull succession of names and dates. But history is made by real people with real passions, shortcomings, and peccadilloes, just like our own. Perhaps not every teacher can bring history alive, but certainly a theme park ought to be able to. I want to get to know those people of the past and their world, and come out changed.

The same applies to technology. There are so many wonderful discoveries being made about space and molecules, our bodies and our environment. Captivate me with such knowledge. I'm certain that with the right story it can be done.

We aren't ignorant fools. It's time theme parks stopped treating us as if we were.

Chapter 60: A Parting Thought

Perhaps if I made three such selfless wishes, the genie would grant me a fourth. If so, here's what I'd wish for all of you:

How much can you accomplish in a year of your life? How about in your entire life? What if I could give you twenty more years of productivity, creativity, self-discovery, and experiences? Moreover, what if I could give you those years starting right now, while you're still young enough to enjoy them? Sounds like a good deal, doesn't it?

There's an easy way you can give yourself those twenty years.

How many hours a day do you watch TV?

All right, I can already hear some of you groaning and saying, "There he goes, getting on his soap box." But bear with me a minute. How many of those hours contain anything of value?

"But I need time to relax," you say. Sure you do, but for how long, and in how vegetative a state?

I heard an interview with Madonna. She has an incredibly full and productive life, combining career, home life, spiritual life, and children. She doesn't watch television, and neither do her kids. When I heard that, I had to revise my whole opinion of her. Now there's someone who's trying to make the most of every moment.

If she can do it, so can you.

If you take back those three hours a day you spend in front of the tube, it's like getting twenty extra years at the office, designing theme parks. Or spent with those you love. Or reading. Or traveling the world. Learning. Doing. LIVING.

Use that time to enrich your mind, your body, or the lives of others. Think what a difference it would make to the world. If you succeed in your quest to become a theme park designer, you will quite literally touch thousands of people's lives each day.

You've already taken the first step by reading this book. From now on it's up to you to make every moment count.

I hope you enjoyed this book. We've covered a lot. I've tried to give you a sampling of every delicacy from the buffet of theme park design, but I'm sure we've overlooked many tasty treats.

If your career plans carry you into this busy and exciting field, drop me a line someday. In this business everyone has a story to tell. I'd love to hear yours.

Perhaps we may even run into each other behind the scenes...

...most likely at 2 o'clock in the morning on opening day.

Now please gather your experiences, passions and inspirations and step into the vehicle. Your ride is just beginning.

About the Author

Steve Alcorn is an entrepreneur, engineer, inventor, author and teacher best known for his involvement in the theme park industry. In 1982 he joined Walt Disney Imagineering (then known as WED Enterprises) as a consultant, where he worked on the electronic systems for Epcot Center. During his time with Imagineering he designed show control systems for The American Adventure, wrote the operating system used in the park-wide monitoring system, and became Imagineering's first Systems Engineer.

In 1986 he founded Alcorn McBride Inc. The company's show control, audio, video and lighting equipment is used in most major theme park attractions around the world.

Mr. Alcorn is the author of several novels and the book *Building A Better Mouse: The Story of the Electronic Imagineers who Designed Epcot*. It's available at themeperks.com.

Through Internet instruction provider ed2go.com, Mr. Alcorn teaches online classes at over 1000 universities and colleges worldwide.

If you enjoyed this book, you might also enjoy the class he teaches in Theme Park Engineering at imagineeringclass.com. It uses this text, and lets you design your own attraction and receive feedback from Mr. Alcorn and other students.

CPSIA information can be obtained at www.ICGtesting.com
Printed in the USA
BVOW042211030912

299505BV00008B/39/P